The Ultimate Guide to Surviving a ZOMBIE Apocalypse

This book is dedicated to my loving and supportive wife. I love you, dear.

The Ultimate Guide to Surviving a ZOMBIE Apocalypse

PALADIN PRESS • BOULDER, COLORADO

F. KIM O'NEILL

The Ultimate Guide to Surviving a Zombie Apocalypse
by F. Kim O'Neill

Copyright © 2010 by F. Kim O'Neill
ISBN 13: 978-1-58160-743-7
Printed in the United States of America

Published by Paladin Press, a division of
Paladin Enterprises, Inc.
Gunbarrel Tech Center
7077 Winchester Circle
Boulder, Colorado 80301 USA
+1.303.443.7250

Direct inquiries and/or orders to the above address.

Cover art by Nathaniel Koffler.

Interior art by Matthew Doyle, Rolf Harding, Jennifer Larson,
Carlos Machuca, Dierdra Olin, and Martin Reimann.

Visit our website at www.paladin-press.com

CONTENTS

What Is a ZOMBIE Apocalypse?

1

A zombie apocalypse is an end-of-the-world scenario in which both social order and government infrastructure have completely broken down as a result of the walking dead wreaking havoc and causing irreparable destruction. While it is true that the notion of apocalypse, or the end of the world, has existed since the beginning of human civilization, a zombie apocalypse is a uniquely horrifying situation that requires a certain set of skills, supplies, and knowledge to survive.

What differentiates a zombie apocalypse from a run-of-the-mill zombie uprising is its duration. A zombie apocalypse is, by its very definition, forever. Its destruction is irrevocable and widespread on a global scale, and it lasts as long as there is a single human brain left to consume. A zombie uprising is temporary, focusing on a small-to-medium number of zombies attacking a single human population, and is typically put down by military means. Every zombie uprising or zombie attack has the potential to turn into a zombie apocalypse if not dealt with in an expedient manner. It is important to recognize the tipping point where a zombie uprising becomes a zombie apocalypse and prepare accordingly.

The information in this book can help you survive a short-term zombie uprising, but the main thrust of this work is the worst-case scenario: there is no cavalry on the horizon coming to save you at the last minute, and you have to live every day in the shadow of the unquiet dead. It is the end of the world as you know it—are you prepared?

WHAT IS THE DIFFERENCE BETWEEN A ZOMBIE APOCALYPSE AND ARMAGEDDON?

For the purposes of this book, we will define Armageddon as the end of the world caused by armed conflict or environmental/natural catastrophe. This can run the gamut of nuclear-war scenarios between superpowers to massive and immediate global warming–caused disasters. It is the setting of movies like Mel Gibson's *Mad Max* and novels like Cormac McCarthy's *The Road*, and it is what most people think of when they consider the term "Armageddon."

One major difference between Armageddon and a zombie apocalypse is that zombies are not known to operate weapons at all, let alone ones powerful enough to destroy large structures. A nuclear-war scenario typically includes the wholesale eradication of major cities and military targets, with the subsequent radioactive fallout from the bombs themselves. This fallout, radioactive dust thrown into the

1

During a zombie apocalypse, both social order and government infrastructure will break down completely. (Illustration by Martin Reimann.)

What Is a ZOMBIE Apocalypse?

atmosphere, can have catastrophically damaging effects on the environment for months, if not years: poisonous rain, cancer-causing agents leaching into the soil, and gigantic ash clouds resulting in years-long nuclear winter. Luckily, in a zombie apocalypse, you won't have to worry too much about that. Some ill-prepared governments may decide to keep a large-scale zombie uprising from becoming a zombie apocalypse through the use of nuclear weapons, but it is not likely that a nuclear-armed country would completely destroy itself in this fashion. Aside from one or two municipalities unwisely destroyed by a nuke-happy military, most cities, towns, and buildings will be relatively intact during a zombie apocalypse. This is a very good thing: scavenging for supplies in abandoned structures will become your new career for quite some time.

Another significant differentiating factor is that you will not only have to compete for resources with your fellow survivors but also have to live under the constant threat of becoming a victim of the walking dead. Zombies don't get tired, give up, or heed pleas for mercy: all they know is hunger and pursuit, which means that your top priority will be self-protection rather than the acquisition of food and shelter. And there will be a lot more of them than there are of you, no matter where you go. History has shown that in times of crisis and civil unrest, individuals don't always band together to cooperatively overcome the threat: in many cases they loot, pillage, rape, and otherwise indulge in their most base desires. Beleaguered and beset by both the living and the undead, you will need to learn a new way to live that puts personal defense before all other concerns.

In addition to the general strain and horror of being alive during the end of the world, when it's likely that many if not all of your friends and family are dead, a zombie apocalypse presents specific psychological and existential concerns that no other Armageddon scenario begins to approach. Imagine having to kill a loved one who, through disease or other process, has become an undead creature bent on clawing you open and eating your brain. Your wife, your child, your best friend: could you do it? Could you stick a gun into Uncle George's once-beloved, now grunting, slobbering, hideous face and pull the trigger? Think carefully, because hesitation kills . . . or worse. The dead won't stay dead. Dealing with these stresses, as well as the terrifying impermanence of not only your survival situation *but also the upending of the concept of death itself,* can be more than some of us can bear.

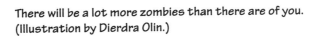

There will be a lot more zombies than there are of you. (Illustration by Dierdra Olin.)

3

One thing to remember about the undead: they won't stay dead, so you'll have to fight them over and over, unless you destroy the brain. (Illustration by Carlos Machuca.)

What Is a ZOMBIE Apocalypse?

WHY DO YOU NEED A BOOK TO SURVIVE A ZOMBIE APOCALYPSE?

Most of you living in the twenty-first century are not prepared to face a basic survival situation, let alone the end of the world. Easy access to refrigerated food, potable water from any spigot, electrically powered machines that do our work for us, and the social compact that keeps most people from murdering each other over petty differences have made modern humanity relatively weak and soft. Today, the driving forces to become physically fit are vanity and the boosting of self-esteem rather than survival. Skills like woodworking, smithing, and weaving are practiced only occasionally as hobbies, and hunting for food is a leisure activity done by people who can still drive a mile down the street to the local McDonald's for a Big Mac if they don't bag any game. The largest cities in America and countries around the world have deliberately disarmed their citizens, making everyone a potential victim of violent predators. This helplessness in the face of true emergency was brought into stark relief in the aftermath of Hurricane Katrina in 2005: many people who couldn't or wouldn't leave the Gulf Coast area during the storm sat and waited after it for the government to rescue them rather than trying to save themselves.

What happens when all of the trappings of civilization are ruthlessly stripped away? The electricity stops running, and there's no easy way to preserve food or get water from the tap. The law of the land becomes the Law of the Jungle: might makes right. Just making it through the day and night depends on the strength of your muscles, the toughness of your will, and the possession of skills that are no longer considered vital to survival. Like it or not, the vast majority of you are simply ill-equipped for this contingency, and when you throw in the extra difficulty of defending yourself against hordes of ravenous zombies, it will be a miracle if you last a week, let alone a month. Your life expectancy has just dropped to next winter . . . if you're lucky.

That's where this book comes in. What will see you through this horrible crisis is not only the knowledge of how to survive but also the confidence such knowledge brings. After reading this book, you will learn:

- The different classifications of zombies, along with their strengths and weaknesses
- How to deal with the overall zombie-caused breakdown of society
- Zombie-fighting tactics and techniques
- How to find food, water, and shelter in a zombie-overrun world
- Skills for dealing with other physical dangers, such as rogue government agencies, zombie animals, and your fellow surviving humans
- How to prepare a zombie bug-out bag today: a kit that will get you through that critical first week of a zombie apocalypse.

Louis Pasteur famously said, "Chance favors the prepared mind." While a cliché, it is no less valid for that, and in this new, terrible world, you will have to make your own luck and be prepared to capitalize on it. With knowledge and skill, practice and a little good fortune, you can survive and even prevail during a zombie apocalypse.

WHY SHOULD YOU LISTEN TO ME?

The clandestine nature of my previous employment has required me to use a pseudonym when writing this text. My relevant background includes 30 years of military service, with more than 10 years of teaching at the U.S. Army's SERE (survival, evasion, rescue, and escape) school; riot control in high-risk environments overseas; and combat in Southeast Asia, the Persian Gulf, and Eastern Europe. After I was sidelined by injury, I took a management position in private security for CERN, the European Organization of Nuclear Research. While a nondisclosure agreement prohibits me from presenting any specifics regarding what I saw during my short tenure there, I can and will say this: the information in this book is more timely and urgent than you can possibly imagine.

Credentials aside, please give this text a thorough read. There will undoubtedly be some things in it that you are already aware of and others you do not believe. Despite that, I urge you to keep an open mind and take what is offered here to heart. This is your survival guide, and it may be the most important book you will ever read. Good luck.

Types of ZOMBIES

In the broadest definition, a zombie is a reanimated corpse that, while able to perform such simple tasks as chasing, eating, and killing people, is nonetheless mostly nonsentient and unable to reason past a very primitive, almost animalistic level. Their *raison d'être* is the consumption of living brain matter, and they will stop at nothing to get it. Other names for zombies include *zombi, the undead, the walking dead, the unquiet dead, ghoul,* and *revenant.* There are three types of zombies, each of which has its own specific characteristics: the viral zombie, the supernatural zombie, and the voodoo zombie.

VIRAL ZOMBIE

Viral zombies are undead creatures created as a result of scientific effort. This typically happens in one of three ways:

- *Scientific Experimentation:* With the sequencing of the human genome, we now know more about the building blocks of life than at any time in recorded human history. For decades, government agencies and privately funded laboratories have been working in the fields of genetic experimentation, human cloning, duplication of body parts, stem-cell manipulation, genetically modified crops, and biomechanical implantation. With this kind of research, a little knowledge can be a very perilous thing, and success can present a much greater danger than failure. Zombies created as a result of genetic experimentation tend to be more grotesque and disturbing in appearance than a run-of-the-mill walking corpse, due to the mutation and warping of once-healthy human tissue.

- *Escaped Virus/Chemical Agent:* Despite international law prohibiting the research and development of biological weapons, supergerms and other vaccine-resistant plagues are still being fashioned for national defense and personal profit. The age-old desire to control one's fellow man has been invigorated by this kind of illegal scientific research, and what started out as a simple mind-control drug may, through accident or design, become something far more terrible. Zombies created through disease tend to be more numerous in the early stages of a zombie apocalypse due to a relatively quick incubation period and ease of pathogen transference. It is a common belief that this type of zombie outbreak is the most likely to occur and become a worldwide problem.

Viral zombies are undead creatures created as a result of scientific effort or mishap. (Illustration by Carlos Machuca.)

- *Extraterrestrial Interference:* With billions of galaxies in the universe, each one housing billions and billions of stars, it would be ludicrous for us to assume that Earth is the only planet in existence with intelligent life. According to the most likely outcomes of the Drake equation—the calculation of how many sentient, potentially communicating civilizations there are in the galaxy—there may be as many as 2,000 intelligent alien species out there. Just as a homeowner might spray pesticide on a beehive to clear his porch of stinging insects, a hostile extraterrestrial force may decide to take this planet for its own by turning its most evolved civilization against itself in an orgy of destruction. This contingency, however farfetched it may seem on the surface, is not something to be ignored. Alien-created zombies are little different from the other kinds of viral undead in terms of appearance and danger to society, but they may be reinforced by alien technology that is impossible to defeat.

SUPERNATURAL ZOMBIE

Supernatural zombies are created through magical or otherwise unexplainable means. While this can include voodoo as the creation agent, the voodoo zombie is a different creature in many respects and deserves its own category. The three ways supernatural zombies can be raised are:

- *Human Magicians:* The New Age Movement (including Wicca, cabalism, ritual magick, and general practice of spirituality through tarot cards, pagan idols, and self-help mantras) has created a huge underclass of amateur magicians. There are many supernatural phenomena that have yet to be properly explained through science, and it very well may be that through the use of magic, the dark arts, or general sorcery,

some committed individuals have managed to pierce, however imperfectly, the veil between the living and the dead. Zombies raised in this fashion can be considered the sorcerous counterparts to zombies created through the error of scientific experimentation.

- *Vampires:* Stories of vampires and vampirism have haunted the nightmares of humankind for millennia, and it is possible that there is a kernel of truth to these ancient legends. Vampires are generally considered to be the princes of the undead, and have many powers and abilities far beyond the ken of mortal men. A common power attributed to vampires is the ability to partially raise the dead to do

Supernatural zombies are created through magical or otherwise unexplainable means. (Illustration by Carlos Machuca.)

Voodoo zombies have been created through incantation and powerful drugs by a practitioner of voodoo. (Illustration by Carlos Machuca.)

their bidding (i.e., create zombies). Vampire-created zombies are extremely frightening because they are under the active control of a hostile entity with particular designs aside from simple death and destruction.

- *Demonic Design:* The rise of postmodernism as a valid philosophy, spirituality over belief in God, and the ascendancy of terrorist death cults in the Middle East have eroded the very fabric of what is good, right, and truthful in human civilization. Many respected eschatologists and Bible scholars have evidence to believe that the End Times are right around the corner. As the world God made turns upside down and inside out, the laws of nature may become more fragile, leading to a zombie apocalypse wrought by Satan himself as a way to spread fear and horror. Demon-raised zombies are typically accompanied by other monsters belched forth from the pits of Hell and stink of brimstone as well as death.

VOODOO ZOMBIE

Voodoo zombies have been created through incantation and powerful drugs by a practitioner of voodoo known as a *bocor*. Brought to popular attention by researcher Wade Davis in his seminal text *The Serpent and the Rainbow*, voodoo zombies are not actually undead creatures, but live humans put into a sorcerous/chemical trance and forced to do the bocor's bidding. It has also been theorized that voodoo zombies are actually hosts for evil, bodiless entities in a Caribbean form of demonic possession. It might not look as though this kind of zombie can become numerous enough to trigger the end of the world, but consider this: there is a great deal of evidence to suggest that government researchers have been studying Haitian bocors for decades to create and standardize their methods of zombie creation. If successful, it shouldn't be too difficult to introduce concentrated zombie powder into a municipal water supply and combine it with subliminally transmitted incantations broadcast over the public airways to create a nation of zombie slaves. Voodoo zombies are usually a little easier to defeat than the other kinds of zombies but are no less frightening and dangerous.

CHARACTERISTICS ALL ZOMBIES SHARE

All zombies, no matter how they were created, share certain characteristics that separate them from the living human populace. In most cases it shouldn't be very difficult to tell a zombie from a normal person, and zombies tend to stick out like sore thumbs in mixed groups. These defining characteristics include:

- *Appearance:* Due to their extremely limited mental capacity and existential condition, zombies have appalling personal hygiene. Their clothes will be ripped, scuffed, and generally dirty. Most zombies also exhibit seeping, bleeding, and suppurating wounds of some kind, including skeletal fractures breaking through the skin, open sores, unhealed gashes, and missing teeth or digits. This is because zombies are extremely clumsy and feel no pain from injuries, so they often bump into things like walls and automobiles, and trip over curbs and other obstacles. Because they are actually dead but still walking around (hence undead), they will stink of blood, rotting flesh, and human waste. Although they do not have to breathe to maintain their nightmarish existence, many zombies make moaning or gobbling noises from their decaying throats, and they almost never speak intelligently. They feel cold to the touch, or at least room temperature, and they do not have a measurable pulse. In fact, the best way to determine the difference between a homeless person and a zombie, *if you need to*, is to take his pulse.
- *Disease*: Zombies attract flies, rats, and other vermin that feed off their putrefying, ambulatory bodies. These insects and rodents may then attach themselves to living hosts and transmit whatever illnesses the zombie, when it was a living person, may have been suffering: HIV, tuberculosis, hepatitis, or other dangerous pathogens. During their travels seeking human brains to eat, zombies may inadvertently infect rivers, streams, and reservoirs, causing the spread of intestinal parasites to those unlucky

individuals who have not properly purified their drinking water. Luckily, there are very few known cases of sexually transmitted diseases jumping from the undead to the living.

- *Horror:* There is something deeply horrifying about the sight of a shuffling, brain-starved undead creature, especially if it used to be someone you knew. Zombies are the very essence of terror and revulsion, from their appalling appearance to their disgusting appetites. Certain psychically sensitive people are able to sense a zombie's proximity before it becomes physically visible, which is a valuable survival trait.

- *Appetite:* Zombies always have a purpose, and, in most cases, that purpose is to eat the brains or bodies of the living. All modern cultures abhor cannibalism, but this taboo no longer applies when you have become one of the hungry undead. The majority of zombie types transmit their horrifying condition through biting, which makes them doubly terrifying: all they want to do is eat you, and, even if they don't succeed, they can still turn you into a one of them with a single bite. This hunger is their only reason to exist, unless being commanded by a more powerful figure, such as a vampire or demon, and they seek to sate their appetites with a single-mindedness that makes them very difficult to overcome.

- *Stupidity:* One of the main things that makes a zombie a zombie, aside from being undead, is its lack of intelligence. Zombies cannot be reasoned with or frightened away, nor will they communicate with you to tell you what they want. They don't have long-term strategies, and their only goal is to consume your brain. Some zombies will attempt to repeatedly perform activities that they habitually engaged in when they were living people, but this is an unfortunate result of neurons misfiring in their rotting gray matter rather than the volition of a thinking mind. The longer a zombie remains a zombie, the more mindless it becomes.

- *Toughness:* The only way to kill a zombie, no matter how it was raised, is to severely injure its brain. Decapitation works to put a zombie down, as does a well-placed bullet or arrow. But it won't stop attacking you if you break its leg or stab it through the heart: it doesn't have a circulatory system that keeps it going. Whatever it is that gives a zombie the ability to shamble and bite and slobber is in its gray matter. Later on in this book you will learn combat techniques specifically designed to defeat zombies, but the rule of thumb is to destroy its brain. Do that, and it turns off like a light switch.

ZOMBIE Apocalypse Basics

The world of the zombie apocalypse will be an alien and terrifying place, despite its earlier familiarity, and you need to know what will happen in it before you can develop a properly working survival plan. Do not put yourself in the mindset of making assumptions as a result of watching Charlton Heston in *The Omega Man* or reading a self-help book on assertiveness and goal development. Understand and acknowledge that the world you once knew has gone completely crazy, and that your survival is based on careful tactical planning rather than what you *think* should work because it worked before zombies overran the world.

The anarchy and lawlessness that are part and parcel of a zombie apocalypse can be at least as disquieting as having to fight the walking dead. The cherished, familiar people who were formerly your friends and neighbors have suddenly become dangerous competition for much-needed resources. When individuals realize that the police are no longer answering 911 calls, theft and looting will become rampant, even in your own neighborhood. In a world with no hope, where the dead literally walk the Earth, "apocalypse fever" will take hold: freed from social and legal restraints, many people will decide that they have nothing left to lose and will act on their basest, most savage impulses. That neighbor who's been complaining about your dandelions spreading to his lawn may decide to settle the score with a .45, permanently. Those hoodlums across the street who've been eyeing your teenage daughter for the last year, the pedophile-looking man who lives alone in a house with the shades perpetually drawn, the camouflage-clad slob with the unkempt yard who has screaming fights with his common-law wife every night: all are potential enemies when the rise of the walking dead breaks the social compact. For equivalent examples, just look at the Los Angeles riots in 1992, the genocide in Rwanda in 1994, and the post-earthquake looting in Haiti in 2010.

People who have the luxury of living in a world where the dead stay quiet in their graves can label justified caution as paranoia, and before you picked up this book, you might have been one of them. You have to look at things through the eyes of someone living in the world of a zombie apocalypse. Your life and your family's lives are now in constant danger: do you trust *any* of these people, the acquaintances you happened to buy a house near, that much? Consider how far you would go to keep your child from becoming a shuffling, drooling, filth-caked dead man's next meal, or worse. Imagine, then, what your next-door neighbor would do to keep *his* kids

During a zombie apocalypse, civilization as we know it will disappear. (Illustration by Jennifer Larson.)

from a similar fate. What *wouldn't* you do? Now take it further: your entire neighborhood. After all, the guy down the street has kids, too. Now the town. All *those* people have to eat. Now the state. What are *they* going to do? And you can hear it right outside your door: the chaos, the screams of the innocent being eaten alive, the groans of the undead as they break through windows to find new victims. The police are dead. The army is overwhelmed. You and your family: that is your new society.

BREAKDOWN OF GOVERNMENT INFRASTRUCTURE

The illusion of civilization with which we have surrounded ourselves can be ripped away in an instant by the broken fingernails of a horde of undead monsters. Municipal employees aren't going to risk their lives at the power plant to make sure you have hot showers during a zombie apocalypse, and your local city council won't hold the line against the zombie threat with writs and meetings and ordinances. We have become very used to a world that gives us instant service and gratification at the flip of a switch, the press of a button, or the turn of a faucet. Public services you will have to learn to do without include:

• *Electricity:* Whether from coal plants, nuclear stations, natural gas, hydroelectric plants, or windmills, the vast majority of us get our electricity from public utilities that require constant care and maintenance to keep them running. It is almost impossible to estimate when you will lose power during a zombie apocalypse. It may be days or even weeks before the power goes out, but go out it will. Permanently. Without electricity, you won't have easy access to refrigeration, light, and heat. Gasoline-powered generators, while useful, also generate a good bit of undead-attracting noise and smoke, and you have to have a constant supply of gas to power

Don't expect to have any electricity—or any other public service—during a zombie apocalypse. (Illustration by Jennifer Larson.)

them. Batteries eventually run out. Hand-cranked radios and flashlights are good in a pinch but not always reliable or very powerful.

- *Water:* When the electricity goes out, it is a good bet that the water will stop running as well. One major concern is that most public water comes from aquifers, reservoirs, lakes, and desalinization plants. Before it gets to your sinks and showers, it goes through a disinfecting and purification process that is powered by electricity. If your water is pumped electrically, it will just stop flowing altogether when the power goes out. If it is pumped through gravity, you may still get water when the electricity shuts off, but it may be unsafe to drink because of the lack of purification and filtering. It is extremely difficult to put a bullet into a zombie's brain when you can barely rise from stomach cramps and explosive diarrhea brought on by drinking bad water.
- *Telephone:* Mobile phones require charged batteries to work, in addition to a network of electrically powered towers to broadcast and amplify signals. At the height of the zombie apocalypse, when the terminally helpless (most of the world) will be calling anyone and everyone for help, for sympathy, for *anything*, your cell phone will become less than useless: discard it and move on. Landlines may last a little longer, but in many places the network will become overloaded with calls for emergency services that will never arrive. Because you have read this book, you will already have a plan in place at the first hint of a zombie attack, so you will not need a phone.
- *Internet:* Email, the World Wide Web, iTunes, and the entire useless network of computers chattering at each other about nothing important will be the first things to come crashing down when the undead rise from their graves to destroy the world. Your Internet Service Provider has better things to do than risk its employees' lives making sure you can download the latest version of *Gears of War.* Zombies don't care about YouTube videos of dogs riding skateboards or the latest episode of *Desperate Housewives.* Out of all the things to be thinking

about during a zombie apocalypse, is your Facebook page *that* important?

INSTITUTING MARTIAL LAW

In the early stages of the zombie apocalypse, at the tipping point just before a widespread zombie attack becomes impossible for the authorities to defend against, it is a safe bet that your government will declare martial law. Polite synonyms for martial law include "state of emergency" and "emergency quarantine," but the effects are exactly the same. Martial law is declared when local authorities are deemed insufficient to maintain basic services and keep the public order during an emergency situation. What happens is that the military takes control of the country, focusing on maintaining security above all else. This is done, of course, with well-trained, heavily armed soldiers, backed up with all the weapons and materials they used to use to defend your country from outside forces. Your personal freedom is now a thing of the past, and you have become subject to the uncompromising statutes of military rule. Living under a state of martial law is difficult enough, but in those critical early days and weeks of a zombie apocalypse, an officially declared state of emergency presents a unique series of dangers that you will need to prepare for.

- *Curfew:* The first thing that will be imposed during martial law is a curfew, which will considerably limit your freedom to move. It is most likely that in the beginning of its imposition, this curfew will last from an hour before sundown to an hour after sunrise. Once the danger of the walking dead grows to epidemic proportions, however, you may be required to stay in your home all day and night while the military tries to deal with the threat. Air raid sirens will usually signal the beginning and end of the day's curfew. Patrolling troops in military vehicles will enforce the curfew, and depending on where you live, the punishment for breaking curfew can range from a warning to imprisonment to summary execution. The military wasn't put in charge to keep you safe: martial law was declared to keep the public order. That means that your individual rights have been severely curtailed, and the military's job is to shoot zombies and potential zombies first and sift through the bodies afterward. When a curfew has been established in your area, your best choice of action is to hunker down and wait for the military to be overrun by the zombie hordes before making your escape. A well-prepared home with reinforced doors and windows, a long-term food and water supply, and plenty of weapons for personal defense will be a safer place to be than dodging both zombies *and* men in jeeps shooting at you because you ran out of Aunt Betty's insulin and had to raid a drugstore after lights-out.

- *Rationing:* The curfew will affect groceries and other retail stores as well as individuals, so supermarkets, gas stations, and pharmacies will be very crowded during the day and locked up tight at night. Deliveries from the warehouses will either be canceled or extremely restricted, meaning that these mobbed stores will have fewer and fewer things to sell. That is when food rationing will begin. The amount and variety of things you can buy will be lessened, and prices will go through the roof. Your locale may institute ration cards in place of money. This might tempt you to begin hoarding food and valuable supplies now, before rationing starts, which is far from a bad thing. But be clever about it: don't buy hundreds of cans of Dinty Moore stew from your local Shop 'n' Save because that will draw unwanted attention. Spread out your purchases. Buy some supplies now at the local store; then drive two towns over and buy some more. Wait a few days before doing this at another place. Before long, you will have a properly stocked pantry ready to nourish you when the entire town goes into lockdown. For God's sake, however, tell *no one* about what you're doing and what you're preparing for, and make dead sure that your family also keeps mum.

At the outset of a zombie apocalypse, one of the first actions of the government will be the imposition of martial law. (Illustration by Dierdra Olin.)

The Ultimate Guide to Surviving a ZOMBIE Apocalypse

During martial law, food hoarders are usually shot and their property is confiscated and distributed throughout the community for the common good. What your neighbors and, more important, *the army* don't know won't hurt them (or you). During a state of emergency, rationing might not be limited to just food. Services like electricity, gas, and water may also be restricted to certain hours to better keep the peace, so prepare to do without if you have to.

- *Transportation:* Where you are allowed to travel will be quite limited once martial law is declared. A perimeter will be established around your town/city/area and patrolled by men with assault rifles. Most nonessential businesses will be closed down: who needs to get a haircut or go to a realtor's open house when cannibalistic undead are shuffling through the streets? Shopping for necessities will be allowed (until it isn't). Medical offices will probably be open, as well as hospitals and drugstores. Unless you're a doctor or supermarket clerk, you will have to have a good reason to be going somewhere during martial law, and if you don't, you can be thrown in jail. Leaving town for any reason will require a permit of some kind. This is why preparing now for a zombie apocalypse is so important: you can't afford to run out of something vital and be unable to get to it because the army won't let you leave town.

- *Internment:* For the sake of maintaining the public order, the military might order everyone into detention camps for the duration of the emergency. Whatever you do, *do not let them take you to a detention camp*: they're absolute death-traps. You will be dependent on the authorities for *everything*: food, water, and your very safety. Don't forget that these are the same authorities who couldn't stop a simple zombie attack from becoming a widespread apocalypse—and they, in fact, might be responsible for the zombies in the first place. What happens when the perimeter is breached and then overrun by the walking dead? How can you defend yourself, let alone your family, when you've been disarmed and thrown into a pen with all the other sheep? When the military begins rounding up your fel-

low citizens to be placed in detention camps "for their own safety," hide in your zombie redoubt and wait for them to leave. They won't spend hours searching your house when they have everyone else in town to gather up and imprison. Once you have avoided capture stay as quiet as possible during both day and night, and do not use any devices plugged into the electrical outlets. Any government authorities monitoring the grid will notice the power use and send teams of soldiers to investigate, and this time they *will* do a thorough job of searching the whole house.

The situation may arise where martial law is declared in your country or city but it is not enforced in your locale. Your country's military is a formidable force, especially against civilians, but its power is finite, and the official lines of communication are likely to break down in a real emergency. This is especially true in rural areas. In that case, locally elected leaders may attempt to take control of all resources and individuals in your area, using law enforcement as a private army. This is very much a worst-case scenario within a worst-case scenario. A military under the control of a centralized government will, at least in the early stages of a zombie apocalypse, act in a way that is consistent with the rule of law. Honor and discipline are respected traits among those who serve, especially in the United States, and soldiers take their responsibilities very seriously. They will be tough but fair. A mayor, city councilman, or local captain of industry who has arrogated power to himself during a national emergency has no such controls. His actions are limited only by his personal sense of ethics, and in his mind, might makes right.

If this should occur, all the rules go out the window, and you have just become a vassal of a tin-pot dictator. Once you see that Mayor Brown is looking to become Warlord Brown, gather whatever supplies you can and flee *immediately*. Fighting zombies *and* a petty tyrant with a private army is a battle you cannot win. This is not just something you can ride out. Your friends and neighbors, hungry for someone to shepherd them through the zombie crisis, will wholeheartedly support their new leader. In the interest of staying on the new master's good side, they'll turn you in as a hoarder and dangerous element in a heartbeat if you attempt to hunker down and wait out the attack in your well-stocked basement. Remember the section on societal breakdown and act in *your* best interests, because everyone else will be doing the same.

YOU'RE ON YOUR OWN

During a zombie apocalypse, self-reliance is the only trait that matters. When everything else has fallen apart, it will be up to *you* to see yourself and your family through the unimaginable terror, danger, and uncertainty: no one else can or will do it for you. As a modern person living in the 21st century, you tend to watch what you do and analyze what you are doing as if from a distance instead of actually being in the moment and *doing* it. You have become a spectator in your own life. Whether this is a consequence of watching too much television or relying overly on machines and contrivances to do the most basic tasks, or simply a consequence of the times in which we live, is immaterial: what matters is that it is up to *you* to become an engaged and active participant in your own life, and if you want to survive the zombie apocalypse, the time to do that is *now*. Don't wait for some future opportunity to gather resources and important information on basic lifesaving skills, because by the time it becomes a priority, your Internet Service Provider will have already been murdered by teeming hordes of the undead.

The army cannot save you and the police won't, so it will be *your* primary responsibility to keep your family from dying of starvation, being raped by roving bands of thugs, or being eaten alive by zombie cannibals. Many of you would like to think that your instincts and skills for self-preservation will suddenly "kick in" when they have to, or that the worst things that can possibly happen won't happen to *you*, but there are mass graves filled with millions of men and women who felt the same way in Stalin's Russia, the Great Leap Forward in China, and Nazi Germany. Expressions like "at all costs" sound dramatic when spoken in polite company at a dinner party, but when you're in the midst of a zombie

apocalypse, those three words have a totemic, almost magical quality: it will be up to *you* to protect yourself *at all costs*. This means that you must be willing to do *whatever it takes* to save yourself, no matter how horrible or distasteful it may seem at the time. If you work at it and make the effort to develop that vital trait of self-reliance, the knowledge of how to keep yourself alive when the world has fallen down around your ears, and the physical skills to defend yourself and your loved ones from all comers, alive or undead, you will prevail.

The proper mindset is key to survival. You can develop this mindset in several ways.

- *Visualization:* When you imagine success as you are confronted with life's challenges, it becomes easier to make that success a reality. When in a crowd or populated area, visualize what might happen if Person A should suddenly become a zombie and begin attacking people at random. What would you do? Have you located and counted the exits? How many people could you put between yourself and the "zombie"? What weapons are you carrying on your person right now? What's nearby that could be used as an improvised zombie-killing tool? Prepare yourself by not just imagining the worst but also figuring out how you would prevail in these scenarios. Be harsh, be realistic, but don't set yourself up for failure, either.
- *Will: Wanting to win* is not the same as *having the will* to win. Building this up requires you to push yourself beyond what you thought your limits could be. Get out of your comfort zone, break through your self-created paradigm, and *challenge yourself*. Every workout you engage in should completely exhaust you: never hold anything back for the return trip. When you play, play hard but honorably. You will never know what you are capable of until you test yourself, and such testing must be as rigorous as possible without creating injury.
- *Hardship:* Knowing how much you can endure is an amazingly empowering thing. Sure, you *think* you can take not eating for several days, but have you actually *tried* it? What about going without sleep? Or making do without a roof

over your head? Or even just going without coffee for a week? Most of us have never had to deal with *true* hardship: starvation, deprivation, utter exhaustion. Getting used to that and knowing what you can take *now* will make it easier to handle when it happens for real.

- *Practice:* Knowledge creates confidence and destroys fear. When you know what to do in an emergency, especially a zombie-created emergency, your chances for survival go up exponentially. But this knowledge must be backed up with true experience in order for it to move from theory to reality. Get out there and *do* the things you've read about. Construct your zombie redoubt and stock it with supplies and weapons you have learned how to use. Practice the combat drills taught in this book. Teach your family the same things that you've learned, because the best way to learn more about a skill is to educate others. Stop being a spectator and start being a doer.

The right survival mindset won't just happen when you want it to, and wishing for things doesn't make them appear. Hope is for people who won't stand up and do what they have to do. Get out there and make your own luck, and the zombies won't make you their next meal.

ZOMBIE Combat Strategies

Now we have come to the heart of the matter: fighting zombies. No doubt many of you have skipped ahead or skimmed through the earlier material to get to this section. Knowing how to defeat the zombie threat is one of the most important skills you will ever learn, but in your zeal to become a slayer of the undead, don't ignore the importance of preparation before you go into action. An often-overlooked aspect of combat is becoming intimately familiar with the circumstances in which you will be fighting. Survival is a holistic effort, encompassing not only combat, but also skill development and marshaling of resources. Keep all of this in mind before seeking combat with the undead.

The definition of combat is fighting against someone who is trying to fight you back, and the very nature of a fight is a struggle. If it were easy, it wouldn't be a fight at all. The longer a fight goes on, the greater your chances for defeat, so you will want to win all your battles as quickly as you can. In the world of the zombie apocalypse, there are no guarantees: every fight can be your last. The police won't be there to break it up before it gets too bad, and the ambulance won't come to patch you up no matter how often you try to call for one.

To successfully and consistently kill zombies, you must learn as much as you can about their strengths and weaknesses, the proper weapons to use, and how to employ good combat tactics. The techniques and strategies laid out here will, if properly practiced, give you the edge that can mean the difference between living out another day in apocalypse and becoming a drooling, undead creature starving for human brains.

ZOMBIE STRENGTHS

Most individual zombies aren't necessarily strong or formidable foes against an armed person committed to his own defense. This doesn't mean that they cannot be deadly dangerous. If you live in a world where a zombie uprising has turned into a full-fledged zombie apocalypse, the zombies have obviously presented a greater danger than could be dealt with by both law enforcement and military forces. Knowing their strengths enables you to mount an effective defense against them.

- *Physical Toughness:* Because zombies aren't subject to the same physical limitations as living humans, they tend to be more resistant to damage. If you cut off a man's hand in a fight, the shock and pain will cause him to stop attacking you, whereas with a zombie, a lost hand is no big deal.

21

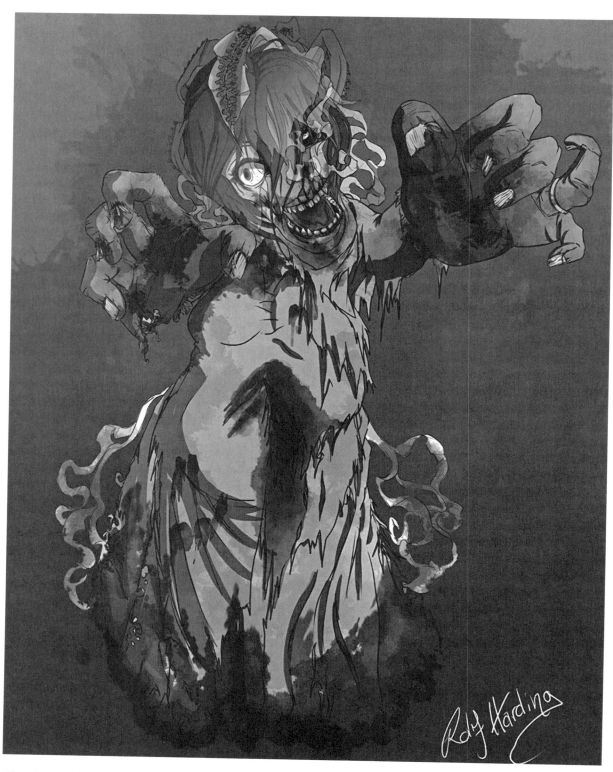

Zombies aren't subject to the same physical limitations as living creatures and are thus more resistant to damage. (Illustration by Rolf Harding.)

It will just thrust the oozing stump at you and keep coming. Because their hearts don't beat, blood loss doesn't affect them. Lactic acid doesn't build in their rotting muscles, so they don't get tired or achy after a long day of hunting humans. You can't inflict pain on dead nerves. Whatever its animating force, a zombie no longer has a connection to what makes a living person work, and as such it follows different physical rules.

- *Mental Toughness:* Zombies cannot think their way past complex problems, but they also do not give up. Ever. They don't experience fear or other similar emotions, and their very single-mindedness is a terrible thing to contend with. A zombie simply will not relent or lose morale, and there is no way to verbally convince one to stop attacking you. In a world where we are taught first to try to reason our way past conflict, the zombie is implacable and deadly.

- *They Come in Groups:* Through accident or instinct, zombies usually travel in packs, and will try to overwhelm you with their numbers. You must learn to be adept at fighting multiple opponents, even entire swarms of them. Shooting one zombie in the head at ten yards is one thing, but what happens when you turn the corner and bump into five of them? Or ten? Or an entire church congregation's worth?

- *They Inflict Disease:* In addition to the diseases the undead usually carry, like bacterial infections from the scratch of their dirty fingernails or cholera-infected fleas hopping from their filthy bodies to yours, most zombies can inflict their horrible condition on you by biting. In some cases, the bite of an infected zombie kills (and half-resurrects) the victim almost instantly, and in other cases it can take a long, agonizing time for you to die and come back as one of them. Either way,

a single bite from a zombie can mean death, whereas a zombie can be sliced and shot many times before deanimating.

- *They Create Horror and Terror:* Most of us would be understandably reluctant to chop the head off of a child, woman, or elderly person, but that hesitation can be deadly in a combat situation. What if the zombie didn't look particularly bloody but instead shuffled at you, making pained, pitiful moaning noises? What if the

Zombies usually travel in packs. (Illustration by Martin Reimann.)

23

zombie once happened to be someone you knew? Someone you loved? So now you have to fight a creature that won't stop attacking you, can kill you with a single bite, is traveling with a group of like-minded monsters, *and* also used to be your beloved Aunt Tess eight hours ago. The degree of horror and terror a single zombie can produce should not be overestimated, and while you may be scared of *it*, it definitely isn't frightened of *you*.

ZOMBIE WEAKNESSES

Despite their many strengths, zombies aren't invincible. They *can* be defeated. There are certain weaknesses inherent in all zombie types that can be exploited to ensure their downfall.

- *They Are Slow and Clumsy:* Zombies are completely incapable of fine motor manipulations, even under the best of circumstances. Only a few rare types of zombies can run, as their lack of a functioning circulatory system keeps them from sprinting any great distances. If you are not surrounded or hindered by unfortunate circumstance, you can usually run away, which makes combat with them a somewhat discretionary thing. They also have trouble navigating stairways and avoiding traps, and often stumble, shamble, and shuffle to get anywhere. This general slowness also keeps them from effectively

ducking, dodging, and avoiding edged weapons or bullets.
- *They Are Extremely Stupid:* Zombies are easily fooled and don't use complicated tactics and strategies to get what they want. They rely on strength of numbers and an indomitable will rather than thinking their way through a problem. Zombies are incapable of switching their focus from one thing to another, and they won't stop trying something simply because it isn't working. They are also very predictable in their appetites and ways to sate them, favoring a simple, direct route over flanking and feinting. What

Zombies are slow and clumsy, which gives you a leg up in a confrontation. (Illustration by Dierdra Olin.)

you see is very much what you get with a zombie.

- *They Don't Use Tools:* While some voodoo zombies may use simple weapons, the rest of them don't fight with guns or swords or cruise missiles. They won't even throw rocks. This means that a zombie's primary danger is at extreme close range: armed, you can usually attack it before it attacks you. The virulence of a zom-

Zombies are extremely unintelligent. (Illustration by Martin Reimann.)

bie's bite only extends to the reach of its teeth. They won't get into a car to chase you down if you run away from them on foot, and they can't call each other on walkie-talkies to triangulate your position. As a living, thinking human, you have far more tools at your disposal than the walking dead, and with some imagination and skill, you can use these tools to your advantage.

CLASSES OF WEAPONRY AND THEIR UTILITY

To get a better grasp on how you can kill zombies, it is helpful to understand, at least in general terms, the kinds of weapons you should and should not use. Most people do not have the familiarity with violence and weapons that the average combat-trained soldier takes for granted, and while zombies no longer have any societal or moral qualms about killing, they themselves always fight unarmed (so to speak).

Edged Weapons

Most edged weapons are intended for close-range fighting, which is far from ideal: you want to take your undead enemy out at as far a distance as possible. Nevertheless, blades require little upkeep aside from occasional sharpening, and never run out of ammunition. They can also do a great deal more functional limb damage to the undead through dismemberment than a firearm: it is easier to chop off an extended arm than it is to shoot it off entirely, and a zombie that is missing an arm has had its combat effectiveness somewhat lessened. In order of size, there are four types of edged weapons:

- *Knives:* Of all four kinds of bladed weapons, the knife is the least useful for killing zombies. Most of the damage a knife inflicts comes in the form of blood loss from slashed arteries, which is fine if you have run up against a living opponent. But as has already been established, zombies do not have a circulatory system that keeps them going. Their rotting hearts just don't beat. The value of a knife in blade combat against the undead increases according to its length, so size *does* matter. With your trusty tactical folder or Granddad's

World War II trench knife, you can slash the skin of the walking dead to ribbons or gut it like a trout, but you won't have stopped it. If your knife is big and heavy enough to cut through an arm or neck in one or two good swings, you might have something there. If not, throw away the knife and go for something bigger.

- *Hatchets and Axes:* Weapons made for chopping work are good for zombie deanimation but not perfect. Heavier than most one-handed swords and with a smaller blade surface, they require some muscle and skill to use effectively in combat. This includes tomahawks, fire axes, trail axes, woodchoppers, and any one-handed weapon that has more handle than blade. The ax is a decent weapon to carry as a backup and is very good as a camp tool, but if you want to become adept with it, practice often and try not to cut yourself on the backswing.

- *Swords and Machetes:* If you have to go into hand-to-hand range with a zombie, the sword is what you'll want to wield. Make sure that you get one with an actual edge on it: fencing foils are next to useless against zombies, and epées do not have the weight and heft to cut off a head or arm. Claymores and other two-handed swords tend to put you a little off-balance and are difficult to redirect in the middle of a swing, which is a huge drawback when fighting multiple undead opponents. A double-edged sword is better than a single-edged blade, but don't turn up your nose at a machete: a skilled machete wielder can chop a group of zombies into quivering chunks of rotten meat in moments.

- *Pole Arms:* This includes spears, halberds, and other blades-on-a-stick like the Japanese *naginata*. They obviously require a great deal of room to maneuver, and if a zombie gets inside your guard (behind the blade at the end of the pole arm and within arm's reach), you're in big trouble. They're also very difficult to carry on a regular basis and impossible to conceal. Overall, pole arms are more trouble than they're worth, and if you should find one on the street, you're better off breaking off the blade and using it as an improvised sword or ax.

Blunt Weapons

Except for the crowbar, which isn't a purpose-designed weapon, blunt weapons lack the utility of blades outside a combat situation. You can't cut vines for an improvised travois with an escrima stick. In a combat situation, they don't do as much functional damage as a *gladius* or .45. A zombie won't stop attacking you because you broke its arm or caved in its ribs. Hence, blunt weapons are far from ideal as undead-killing weapons but not *entirely* useless. For our purposes, blunt weapons will be classified in two ways:

- *Bludgeons:* Bats, quarterstaffs, cudgels, sticks, tetsubo, hammers, and anything else that makes a thump when you hit with it. They are very good when dealing with living opponents, as the pain, trauma, and stunning effect of being hit hard with a club or tactical baton can be fight-stoppers. Zombies cannot be stunned or otherwise rendered unconscious, however, and unless you hit them hard enough to not only crush the skull but also cause significant brain damage by pulping the gray matter, all you'll be doing is tiring your arms. It is possible to slow a zombie down somewhat with a good swing of, say, an aluminum softball bat, but your intent as a zombie killer is to permanently deanimate your opponent.

- *Flexible Weapons:* Ropes, cables, nets, and cords. Zombies don't breathe, so they cannot be asphyxiated. A skilled assassin can decapitate a zombie with a length of piano wire wrapped around the throat, but that process takes much longer than it does to just hack off its head with a machete or hatchet. With a lot of practice you can temporarily bind or immobilize a zombie with a lasso, but you haven't eliminated it. A net can entangle several zombies at once, but nets are heavy and unwieldy to carry for any length of time. Leave the ropes for setting up a tent or garroting a head of state: don't rely on them to defeat a zombie.

Projectile Weapons

This class includes any handheld distance weapon that is not a firearm. Unfortunately, very few projectile weapons are useful in zombie combat.

To bludgeon a zombie into submission, you must hit it hard enough to cause significant brain damage. (Illustration by Dierdra Olin.)

Consider that the reason people fight with weapons at all is because they make larger holes that let the body's blood out more easily than empty hands are capable of doing. Projectile weapons simply seek to do this at a distance. We already know that zombies don't bleed out: they die when decapitated or subjected to catastrophic brain injury. As such, most projectile weapons cannot be depended upon to do this task. The types of projectile weapons we will discuss are:

*   *Thrown Weapons*: Thrown knives, axes, spears, and bolas. To distract or wound a living person, a throwing knife is an excellent tool. The difficulty in using one against a zombie is that you have to throw hard enough to not only pierce the skull, but also significantly damage the brain inside. Or, during the chaos and movement of a real fight, you must be skilled enough to launch the knife into a zombie's eye socket (and hence penetrate into the brain). The same goes for spears, javelins, and darts, though an atlatl or similar launcher can greatly enhance your projectile's velocity. Throwing axes are large, difficult to carry in sufficient quantity, and unreliable when it comes to targeting and zombie-stopping power. A bola is only good if you're looking to trip a zombie, otherwise it's as useless as any other flexible weapon. The other considerable drawback to thrown weapons is that they all require lots and lots of space and time to achieve good combat accuracy. Throwing knives is fun, but it is not a skill that will save you in a zombie apocalypse.

*   *Bows and Arrows:* While it takes a great deal of practice to get good at it, a skilled archer can be almost as effective a zombie killer as a good rifleman. A bow may be more easily acquired in some locales than a pistol or carbine, and it has the advantage of relative silence (zombies are attracted to loud noises like the report of a gunshot). The only worthwhile target with a bow is the head, otherwise you're just turning the zombie into a shambling pincushion. A sharpened arrow point propelled accurately by a quality bow can punch right through a skull and scramble an undead brain.

*   *Slings:* From slings to slingshots. A slingshot is a Y-shaped handle with an elastic band and cup strung across the top, while a sling is just a length of cord with a cup that holds a stone. The term for a projectile that is launched from a sling is a bullet. These definitions have been provided for you so that you'll know what to avoid when fighting zombies, because slings are worthless against the undead. This includes the staff sling, which is a one- to two-meter staff with a loop on the end for throwing a bullet, not entirely unlike a lacrosse stick. These weapons simply do not develop enough force to do deanimating damage to the undead.

Firearms

There is something about a gun that captures the attention in a way no other weapon can. A missile is huge—too big to take in all at once. Swords and knives are frightening but only at close range. A firearm, however, can bring death at very long distances and to multiple opponents in a very short period. Regardless of your personal feelings about violence, gun control, and the media-fueled terror most of you have been socialized into experiencing at the thought of defending yourself with a firearm, during the zombie apocalypse a working gun will be your best friend. With some practice and plenty of ammunition, you can ensure your safety with a firearm better than you can with just about any other weapon you can get your hands on. If you are unlucky enough to live in a place where your access to firearms ranges from limited to nonexistent, your best bet is to invest in a good longbow and lots of arrows. For everyone else, read on. There are five main types of firearms that will be discussed in this text:

*   *Handguns:* The two kinds of handguns are revolvers and semiautomatics. Questions of caliber, round capacity, and marksmanship aside, a handgun is an exceptional weapon for close- to medium-range zombie killing. Once you get past thirty yards, the handgun begins to lose its effectiveness, but at zero to ten yards you can stack zombies like cordwood.
    *   ◆ *Revolvers:* The main advantage to using a

A handgun is for close- to medium-range encounters. Past thirty yards, it is useless against zombies. (Illustration by Dierdra Olin.)

Never go full-auto in a fight with the undead. (Illustration by Rolf Harding.)

revolver is that it is far less likely to jam in a combat situation. The drawback is that revolvers don't have the round capacity of pistols, and most carry between five and eight rounds in the cylinder. Unless you are in a cowboy movie, stay away from single-action trigger revolvers, as they require that you manually cock the hammer back after each shot to keep working.

◆ *Semiautomatics:* The freedom of a larger magazine capacity (some long magazines can hold sixteen or seventeen rounds) gives you more shots before reloading, but you must balance that against the stronger likelihood of the weapon jamming in a fight.

- *Machine Guns:* This class includes large military-grade machine guns, such as the U.S.-made M60, and submachine guns, such as the popular Heckler & Koch MP5 and the Israeli Uzi. M60s, Browning M2s, and other heavy machine guns are difficult for most civilians to obtain and usually require a tripod to work properly. Submachine guns, such as the MP5, are easier to purchase and carry, and have lighter caliber ammunition. What makes a machine gun a machine gun is, in part, its ability to shoot on full auto and hence throw a great deal of lead downrange very quickly. So the longer you hold down the trigger, the longer it will continue to fire. In many places around the world, including the United States, it is illegal to privately own a weapon capable of going fully automatic. Most machine guns don't have the option of shooting full auto. Hence, if you own a machine gun and want to make it fully automatic, you must illegally modify it. Do not do this: while it is a lot of fun to just spray bullets everywhere, it is inaccurate and extremely wasteful of ammunition.

- *Shotguns:* Don't depend on the farmer's double-barreled shotgun, as its limited round capacity and rate of fire don't compare to an automatic or pump shotgun designed for actual combat. A varmint gun is good in a pinch, but upgrade as soon as you can. In addition to dealing out hot death to the undead at close to medium range, shotguns also have the advantage of jamming

less frequently than machine guns and semiautomatic pistols. Shotgun ammunition comes in three types: birdshot, which is only useful at very close range; buckshot, which consists of larger pellets that do greater damage at longer ranges; and the tactical slug, which is one large chunk of lead that can explode a zombie's diseased head like a rifle round. An automatic shotgun, such as the Mossberg 935, expels the empty shells when fired, making the weapon ready to shoot immediately. Pump shotguns, like the popular Remington 870, requires that you rack the fore-end back to eject the spent shell and insert a fresh cartridge into the chamber, and then push it forward to put the firing pin into position (also called "pumping," hence the term "pump shotgun"). Most shotguns don't have the round capacity of a good semiautomatic pistol but can carry up to eight. The recoil can be painful and difficult to manage at first, but the damage they can do to the undead more than makes up for it.

- *Assault Rifles:* Like shotguns, assault rifles are shoulder weapons—long guns that require both hands to manipulate effectively in combat. They have detachable magazines that can hold dozens of cartridges and are the weapon of choice for infantrymen in most armies across the globe. They are good from short to very long range but at extreme close quarters can be more difficult to employ than a handgun. Due to the rifling and length of barrel, the bullets that come out of a quality assault rifle are far more lethal than from a handgun or most machine guns. The most common assault rifles you will encounter are the Russian-made AK-47, beloved by third-world combatants everywhere, and the American-made AR-15, which is still in use by the U.S. military under the designation M16. The rates of fire for an assault rifle are single shot, where one pull of the trigger releases a single bullet; burst shooting, where one pull of the trigger releases two or three bullets in very quick succession; and automatic fire. Like machine guns, it is illegal in most countries for civilians to own and use an assault rifle that has been modified to allow automatic fire.

- *Sniper Rifles:* Best at extreme long range, a sniper rifle launches death at around 800 to 1,000 meters per second, and usually the zombie never hears the shot that explodes its skull. A skilled sniper in a good hide can near-invisibly take out dozens and dozens of the walking dead in relative safety. To be a good sniper, you need to have elite skills in camouflage, marksmanship, and patience.

Chemical and Electrical Weapons

Weapons like mace, oleoresin capsicum (also known as pepper spray), nerve gas, insecticide, or any other chemical agent that can bother, annoy, slow down, or even kill a living person will have little to no effect on the undead. This includes most acids that you will be able to get your hands on, as they take too long to have good effect in a combat situation. A blinded zombie can still hear and perhaps smell you, and will just keep coming. Think of an enemy strong enough to withstand the trauma of not only dying but also coming back from the dead: a chemical burn isn't going to stop it, and you can't make it run away or do much more than make its eyes water with that can of pepper gas you've been carrying in your purse for the last few years.

Tasers and stun guns are likewise ineffective. A Taser creates a stunning effect by overloading a living body's nervous system with a jolt of electricity, causing agonizing muscle spasms, temporary immobility, and even mental confusion. A zombie's nervous system no longer works the way it did when it was a living person, and its musculature is no longer controlled entirely by electrochemical nerve impulses. The most you can do with a Taser is cook its skin a little or give it a charley horse in the spot you've shocked it. High-voltage power lines might do the trick, but if you remember from Chapter 3, the power is most likely going to go out by the time this becomes an issue.

Weapons to Avoid

Knowing what you *should* do is vital to success, but you also need to know what *not* to do to keep from making the kind of mistake you can't come back from. In addition to small knives, slings, ropes, electrical and chemical agents, and any other weapon that won't cause either catastrophic brain

injury or mobility-affecting harm, here is a short list of weapons that you should not rely on when facing the zombie threat.

- *Crossbows:* Somewhat fragile since the firing mechanism is out in the open, even the most modern crossbow is not as reliable as a good longbow. The manual models take an unacceptably long time to reload after the first shot, and the magazine-fed kinds are more likely to jam than a semiautomatic handgun. The velocity of bolts (also called quarrels) shot out of a modern crossbow is greater than that of a longbow, but the longbow arrow's weight gives it a better overall punch than a crossbow bolt. The advantage to a crossbow is its relative ease of firing compared to a bow. If you have absolutely nothing else at hand, you may have to make do with a crossbow, but otherwise try to find something better for that long-range attack.
- *Molotov Cocktails and Flamethrowers:* Fire cleanses, but zombies aren't afraid of it. To have any effect, you'd have to burn the zombie long enough to boil or fry the brain inside its skull, which can take a very long time in the heat of hand-to-hand combat. And where are you going to get hold of a flamethrower and enough fuel to keep it going for an appreciable length of time?
- *Brass Knuckles and Pocket Sticks:* If you've read the section on blunt weapons, then you'll already know that just beating on a zombie is no good unless you're doing functional leg or brain damage to it. Small blunt instruments are force multipliers, yes, but only against living beings. You can knock a zombie's teeth out, break its jaw, or pulverize its rib cage, but you haven't notably altered its combat effectiveness. The other danger in these kinds of weapons is that they require you to be very up close and personal with the zombie and its disease-carrying teeth, whereas with a gun or even a sword you can do a lot of damage at greater distance. In combat as well as football, inches matter.
- *Mixed Martial Arts:* Zombies don't tap. You can't choke out a zombie, no matter how tight your rear naked strangle is. The grappling arts are very popular these days, but don't let their

You can't choke out a zombie, so the grappling arts are useless against the undead. (Illustration by Jennifer Larson.)

apparent utility against a living person fool you. Unlike the octagon, there are no rules in zombie combat, and there won't be a referee that will stop the fight when your undead opponent starts biting your skull open to get the gray matter within. Also consider that while you're rolling around on the ground trying to get an arm bar on a zombie, his hungry ghoul buddies will be falling all over themselves to get at you.

Improvised Weapons

If, for whatever reason or circumstance, you find yourself facing a zombie without the benefit of a purpose-designed weapon, you will have to improvise. Don't ever go unarmed if you don't absolutely have to. Almost anything around you can be used as an improvised weapon as long as you have the will and imagination to recognize it. As an experiment, take a look around the room you're in and identify some potential weapons: the telephone over there could be used to knock someone out, the pen on your desk could be jammed into an eye to blind someone, and even that bottle of water could be thrown into an attacker's face to momentarily distract him so you can flee or find something better. The vast majority of improvised weapons can only inflict minor or momentary trauma, which as we already know won't bother the undead. To reiterate, the best weapons are those that will damage the zombie's brain or significantly hamper its mobility. With these two simple rules, take a look around the room again and re-evaluate. Your chances don't look so good any more, do they?

The best solution to the improvised weapons problem is to never go unarmed. Take the threat of a zombie attack seriously, and you will never have to worry about how you would fight off a horde of hungry undead with a stapler, a coffee cup, and your Blackberry.

BLADE COMBAT WITH ZOMBIES

If you have to go hand-to-hand with a zombie, even with an edged weapon, it means everything else has gone wrong for you that day. You didn't notice the zombie from a distance and avoid it entirely, you couldn't flee from it on foot or in an automobile, and you couldn't deanimate it at a distance with a gun or projectile weapon. Despite this, fighting with a sword or machete is much better than trying to kill it with a blunt instrument and worlds better than just punching and kicking the thing.

Selecting the Right Weapon

Going on the aforementioned principle of bigger is better when it comes to edged weapons, swords are preferable to knives, but you don't want to go *too* long. A heavy two-handed sword like the Scottish claymore or German *grossemesser* may *look* impressive, but you won't scare the undead with it, and after the first decapitating swing, it's extremely difficult to reorient and bring the weapon back to bear when you're

fighting multiple zombies. A light, fast blade like a fencing saber can deliver many gashes and cuts, but probably won't shear through undead vertebrae to get the kill. Whichever edged weapon you choose, make sure that you're comfortable with it in hand and that you are confident that you can use it to save your life in an apocalyptic undead emergency. Criteria for edged-weapon selection are:

- *Size:* The ideal blade length is approximately 12 to 36 inches—long enough to hack through an outstretched arm or undead neck in one or two good blows but not so heavy that it becomes unwieldy after a few moments. If you go much shorter than that, you run the risk of getting closer to the zombie than you might like; if you go longer, you will need more room to swing it effectively. As zombies prefer fighting at extreme close-quarters to employ their

The first lesson of blade combat is don't cut yourself. (Illustration by Martin Reimann.)

pathogen-ridden bites, you want to be able to control the range. Your blade must also be light enough to move rapidly but heavy enough to cut through clothing, rotting flesh, and bone without breaking or worse, bouncing back at you. One-handed blades are preferable to two-handed swords: a practiced fighter can chop with one hand and shoot with the other to dispatch multiple undead assailants.

- *Shape:* Curved or straight? A curved sword like a Japanese katana or cavalry saber can create some very devastating flesh wounds, but that's not what we're after in combat with the walking dead. We want to cut *through*, not just slash. The curvature of a saber-like weapon informs that weapon's fighting style, which opens flesh and lets blood out. This is perfect when fighting living humans, but we know that zombies don't die from blood loss. What you want is a straight blade, something that hacks through or splinters heavy bones, such as the humerus or skull. The only exception to this rule is the kukri, the preferred edged weapon of the Nepalese Gurkha soldiers. The shape of the blade is unusual: it is *bent*, with the cutting edge on the inside of the bend. This makes it an exceptional zombie-killing weapon because it delivers a massive amount of cutting force along a small, keen area. There are legends of Gurkhas decapitating living cows with such a blade, so if it can do that, it can certainly deanimate a zombie with a little less effort.

- *Edge:* Your blade should be sharp but not *too* sharp. The thinner your edge, the more likely it is to bend, blunt, or notch when hacking through a skull or neck bone. Machetes are excellent for killing zombies, but they are limited by the single edge and lack of an aggressive point. Two edges are better than one: another edge just gives you more opportunities to cut the enemy, even incidentally. An accidental dismemberment is still a good shot. Your weapon should also have a point, but one that isn't too tapered and, hence, fragile. You want to be able to jam it into the thinner bones of the upper face and temple without it bending or breaking off.

All things considered, the kukri is the blade of choice among the discerning zombie killer: it has an aggressive stabbing point, and it is small enough to be wielded very quickly but heavy enough to do combative dismembering and decapitating with relative ease. Failing that, the Roman *spatha* or slightly shorter *gladius* is an excellent follow-up selection.

Targets with Bladed Weapons

If the only way to kill a zombie is to inflict catastrophic brain injury, it stands to reason that the best place to cut a zombie is the head and neck region. It is important to note that some zombies won't immediately die when beheaded, especially the supernatural variety. Viral and voodoo zombies are more likely to deanimate upon decapitation, so your targeting will have to depend, in part, on the kind of creature you're fighting. The older and more decayed a zombie is, the more brittle its bones become, and if you're up against one that is missing a good amount of flesh on its skeleton, your targeting can become that much easier.

- *Head:* The skull is a difficult bone to cut through, but if you can do it and slash through the brain inside, it's an instant kill. The only reason to hack at the head is to damage its brain, so don't deliberately try to cut off its lower jaw or slash across the eyes: it can still smell and hear you even if it can't see you, and without a lower jaw it can still rake at you with its upper teeth. The thinnest area of the skull is in the upper part of the face: the "T" shape of the eyes and nose. A good, hard thrust through there has a decent shot of penetrating the bone and shearing into the brain. You might be tempted to try to go under the jaw for a thrust upward into the brain from below, but it's a difficult shot and increases the risk of getting your blade stuck inside its head for the precious few moments you might need to attack another undead assailant. Note that you may also get your edge caught in the cleft of even a very good chop through the top or side of the skull, so adjust accordingly.

- *Neck:* Decapitating a zombie is usually an instant kill. Despite the relatively small surface area of the vertebrae, a zombie's neck doesn't move that much. This is a target chiefly for cutting rather than thrusting, so the edge will be the part of the blade you must apply to have effect. You may not be immediately successful with the first hit: even decaying muscle and bone have significant mass to cut through. Hence, a proper beheading may require a few good chops. The perfect place to cut is between C6 and C7 of the cervical vertebrae. Aim lower, and in the heat of battle you may miss and cut impotently at its chest. Aim higher, and your blade can accidentally bounce off the chin or get caught in its jaw.

- *Arms:* Zombies will mindlessly try to grab you and pull you in for that fatal bite, so the arms and hands are decent targets to hit. Consider, though, that hacking off a zombie's arms is only a delaying tactic, not a killing technique: armless undead are still hungry for your brain. Because they will be extended and coming at you, arm and wrist cuts will be easier to pull off than neck shots, but don't get so caught up on whacking off arms that you forget to do the coup de grâce to the neck or head. Go for its forearms and wrists rather than its upper arms: the smaller, thinner bones of the radius and ulna are easier to cut through than the thicker bone of the humerus. A perfect dismembering hit would be right at the joints of the wrist or elbow so you don't have to hack twice or more through bone, but in the chaos of a real fight against a determined undead attacker, such a strike can be very difficult to pull off.
- *Torso:* There are no killing, stopping, or delaying strikes available in the upper torso and thorax, so don't waste the effort stabbing or chopping into that region. You can let a zombie's green-gray guts out of its undead abdomen with a perfect slash across the belly, but all the monster will do is stumble a little bit on its own entrails as it continues after you. Stab it through the heart, and you can get your blade firmly caught in its rib cage. The effort it would take to hack all the way through its abdomen between the ribs and hip, severing the spine, is not worth it.

- *Legs:* You can limit a zombie's mobility by hacking through its femur, but the strength required to do that is better served by going for a higher neck or skull shot. Even completely legless, a zombie can still crawl after you, and a bite on the ankle can be just as fatal as a bite on the neck and shoulder. For bladed combat, striking at the legs is a low-percentage tactic that can leave you open for high-line bites, so save your hits for the arms, neck, and head.

Techniques for Fighting with Edged Weapons

Now that you know *what* to hit, you should learn *how* to hit. Zombie-killing flow drills that are designed to burn functional combat movements into your muscle memory will be described in detail in Chapter 7. For now, here are some things that will be useful to know should you find yourself facing zombies while armed only with an edged weapon.

Cutting Techniques

Your most effective undead-killing movements will all occur above the waist; we've already discussed how going for the legs is mostly a waste of time.

- *Horizontal Forehand Strike:* This strike is aimed at the neck. With some practice and a little muscle behind it, you can effect a decapitation in one or two blows. To do it, hold the weapon horizontally, blade over your shoulder, and swing the weapon in a horizontal arc, edge parallel to the ground. When the weapon reaches your opposite elbow, roll your wrist over to set yourself up for a good backhand shot.
- *Horizontal Backhand Strike:* Also aimed at the neck, this strike is typically performed when you have either cut all the way through your target or missed entirely. It is a little less strong than the horizontal forehand strike but can be very useful in hacking through that last half-inch of bone after a good but not entirely successful forehand. In performance, swing the weapon back horizontally and, just before you hyperextend your elbow, roll your wrist and bring the blade back over your shoulder.

Horizontal forehand (left) and backhand strikes. (Illustrations by Rolf Harding.)

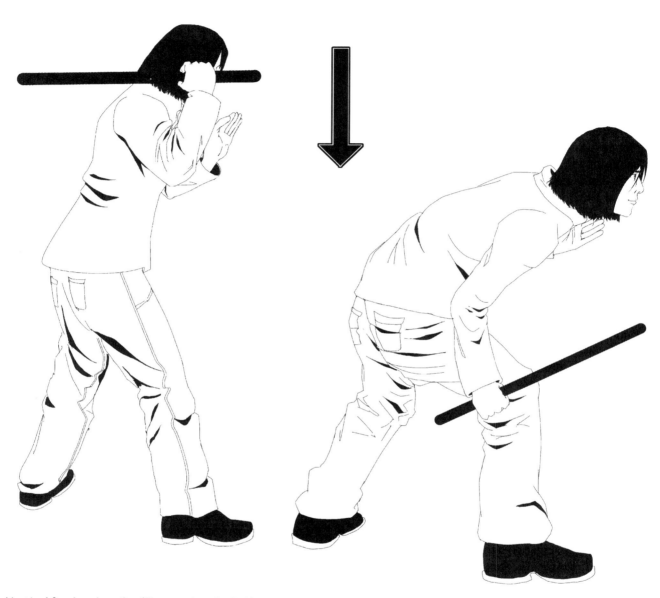

Vertical forehand strike. (Illustrations by Rolf Harding.)

• *Vertical Forehand Strike:* This strike is ideal for hacking down into a skull or, with a little cant to your wrist, cutting off an extended hand or arm. To perform it, start with your weapon held horizontally with the blade over your shoulder. Slice down and *through* the target, dropping your body weight to add force to the blow. In a cycling movement of your arm, bring the weapon back to the starting position.

Thrusting Techniques

The only decent target with a thrust is the face or temple. A thrust to the temple is a tricky, difficult shot to pull off, as you're very likely to miss and overextend yourself or just bounce the blade's point over and across the skull.

• *Forehand Thrust:* To perform this thrust, start with the blade low and at your hip, point facing forward. Your strong-side leg should be back. As you thrust the blade out, step forward and turn your wrist at a 45-degree angle to develop the maximum force from your arm, shoulder, and hips. Even with the angle, this strike can pierce the thin parts of a zombie's face with relative ease.

Forehand thrust. (Illustrations by Rolf Harding.)

• *Straight-Line Thrust:* Starting in the same position as for the forehand thrust, step forward and lean or even vault into the target as you jam the

weapon's point straight out. It requires a little more finesse than the forehand thrust, but with practice it is just as effective.

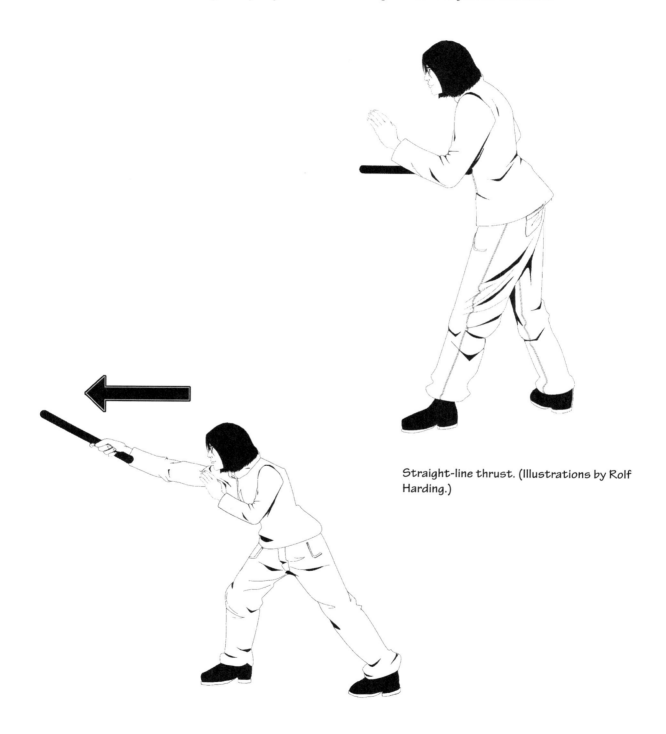

Straight-line thrust. (Illustrations by Rolf Harding.)

- *Backhand Thrust:* There are two ways to perform this attack. To do it the first way, begin at the same starting position as for the forehand thrust, and when you step forward, thrust the point out as you roll your wrist so that your palm is facing the sky. Try to jam the point of your blade as far out as you possibly can to achieve the most force. The other way is to do this attack after a horizontal forehand strike. With your blade already over your opposite shoulder, turn your palm to face the sky and thrust it forward. One of the main advantages of this attack is that it comes from a surprising angle, and the amount of penetrating power you can develop is very respectable.

Backhand thrust. (Illustrations by Rolf Harding.)

Chopping

A chop is simply a cut that stops short after it hits the target so that you can quickly withdraw the weapon and make follow-up chops. This is how axmen cut down trees. The problem with chopping is that, if your concern during the cut is to stop the momentum at the end, you will not bring the maximum amount of force to bear upon your target. You'll slow it as you penetrate, which will result in a less effective cut. When attacking with a blade, always try to cut all the way *through* whatever it is you're hitting. A wounded zombie is still a dangerous foe.

Self-Injury

Do *not* cut yourself. One of the main reasons why people chop instead of cut is because they are afraid of slicing themselves open in the follow-through of a good, strong cut. The best way to avoid cutting yourself is, simply, to not cut yourself. Be aware of what your body is doing and, perhaps more important, be aware of where the cutting edge of your blade is at all times. The easiest way to do this is to practice these movements over and over until they become second nature. Don't wait until plague-infested zombies are pounding on your front door to begin performing the cutting and thrusting techniques described here.

Stay Mobile

While fighting with an edged weapon requires you to get into fairly close range with a mindless undead monster starving for your brains, you do have a slight advantage. The length of your arm and blade allows you to do lethal damage at a longer distance than the zombie, who has to get very close to bite you. Work on controlling the range with footwork and body angling to keep the zombies at bay while you hack at anything that comes into your kill zone. Don't think that you always have to fight head-on, either: stepping diagonally out of line (called *in-quartata*) to hack at your enemy's neck makes the zombie have to turn and reorient its body to face and attack you. Given enough room, you can literally run circles around your slower, clumsier adversary.

ATTACKING ZOMBIES WITH BLUNT WEAPONS

Fighting a zombie with a blunt weapon is only slightly better than attacking it with your bare hands. It is extremely difficult to inflict enough structural damage to its limbs with a baton or staff, and crushing its skull might not do enough damage to the rotting brain inside to end its miserable existence immediately. Thing is, you may be caught short and only have a blunt instrument at hand if you find the undead crawling through your bedroom window, so keep the following in mind:

Weapon Selection

The temptation will be to go big when selecting a blunt weapon: more weight equals more damage. Sledgehammers can indeed inflict some truly devastating wounds, but they are extremely unwieldy in a combat situation. The sledgehammer's head tends to drag you off balance even after a good swing, and recovery to a proper fighting position can be slow even for a strong person. The best blunt instrument for zombie deanimation is the claw hammer: it is relatively fast, delivers a decent amount of skull-cracking force across a small surface area, and the claw end can be used to dig into a wound and widen it further. Tire irons and crowbars are almost as good and about as easy to find.

Targets with Blunt Weapons

Obviously, the only decent target for a hammer-type weapon is the skull. Unfortunately, even a really good, solid hit won't necessarily do enough damage to the zombie's deliquescing gray matter to kill it in the way a proper beheading with a sword might. Hence, several strikes to the top or side of the head will be necessary. This is very problematic in that if you have to hack several times in the same place on the same zombie's head, you are tiring yourself out, wasting valuable time, and leaving yourself open for attacks from its undead comrades.

Striking Techniques

There are four techniques that can be used to inflict zombie-stopping damage with a blunt weapon. They each need to be done full-force for them to work, otherwise you're just Rolfing its rotting muscles.

- *Horizontal Forehand Strike:* The performance of this strike is exactly the same as for the bladed version, except that you will get more bounce-off than you would with an edged weapon. Aim for the temple and strike multiple times.
- *Horizontal Backhand Strike:* This is also the same as the bladed version, though less useful. You cannot derive as much power from the backhand as you can with a forehand strike, and with a blunt weapon, force is everything. Use it as a clearing action so you can return to the less futile horizontal forehand strike.
- *Vertical Forehand Strike:* Once again, this is just like the vertical forehand strike described in the edged-weapon section. Aim for the forehead or top of the skull with this strike, being mindful of the likelihood of rebounding if the zombie you're fighting is relatively fresh (that is, was a living human not too long ago). Do not perform this strike if your undead opponent is significantly taller than you, for obvious reasons.
- *Break-and-Pull:* This technique is used with a claw hammer or crowbar. After performing one or two successful (but not lethal) vertical or horizontal forehand strikes in the same place with the business end of the weapon, rotate your wrist so that the claw end is forward. Thrust it into the broken, splintery hole in the zombie's skull, keep it there, and grab hold of your weapon-carrying wrist with your free hand. Using your entire body weight, pull the zombie off balance toward your opposite shoulder, let go of both the weapon and your own wrist, and run away through the gap your technique has created.

Mobility

If you don't absolutely *have* to face a zombie or horde of zombies while armed only with a hammer or bludgeon as your primary weapon, *don't do it.* There's no shame in running away to find a better weapon, and it's not as if the zombies are going to think less of you because you fled. Practice your break-and-pull technique and always seek the path

to escape when engaged in blunt weapon combat with the walking dead.

ZOMBIE GUNFIGHTING

Killing a zombie from the distance a firearm affords is always preferable to closing distance with it, fighting it hand-to-hand, and running the risk of being infected by its pathogen-ridden bite. You don't need to be particularly strong or athletic to shoot zombies, though some physical strength (especially in the hands) and speed are very useful attributes to have in any survival situation. The preceding sections have already described the general characteristics of most firearms available to the civilian, so what will be described here are some all-purpose firearm rules and techniques specific to certain firearm types.

General Shooting Strategies

There is a lot more to shooting and getting good hits on target than just pointing a gun and pulling the trigger, and this text is not intended to be a primer on basic gunhandling. Becoming a good shot takes practice, persistence, and an intimate familiarity with not only the characteristics of the gun you're shooting, but also the kinds of conditions in which you will be forced to fire. Despite the multitude of firearms and shooting situations, there are some tactics common to gun combat in general:

- *Use the Sights:* The sighted fire vs. point shooting debate among combat shooters is one that will probably persist after zombies have eaten the last living brain on Earth. Sighted fire is exactly what it sounds like: you put the sights on the target and pull the trigger. Point shooting utilizes the body's natural instinct to accurately hit what one is pointing at without using the sights. It can be a very effective technique when you are facing at close range a living person, who can be stopped or killed with shots to the torso, but when it comes to deanimating the walking dead, the best shots are to the head. If you want to get accurate, zombie-killing shots to the head at a distance, you will need to use the sights. Getting on the sights every time you bring the weapon up takes practice, but it's worth it: you don't want to just point shoot all the time and *hope* you can blow the zombie's brains out. The only situation in which you wouldn't want to use the sights and instead point shoot is at extreme close range, where the zombie is near enough to grab your gun. In that case, if you cannot run, then you will have to bring the weapon closer to you, point it in the right direction, and shoot until you can gain distance to once again use sighted fire.

- *Don't Worry About Stance:* The other great debate among firearms enthusiasts is the shooting stance for a handgun: the Weaver stance vs. Isosceles. To shoot Weaver, you keep the gun arm straight while your support arm is bent downward to create muscular tension, which will minimize recoil. The Isosceles stance is where both arms are straight out in front of you, elbows slightly bent, and gun flip from recoil is minimized by your skeletal alignment. In a real fight for your life against the unquiet dead, this debate is a gigantic waste of time: if you can get good headshots shooting Weaver, do it. If you can quickly get on the sights and blow zombies away using Isosceles, go for it. Just pick one and practice it over and over until it becomes second nature.

- *Shoot One Bullet at a Time:* If you are armed with a weapon capable of going fully automatic, the panic and chaos of a gunfight may tempt you to sling as much lead as fast as you can downrange to eliminate the threat, a tactic called "spray and pray." Obviously, if you are doing this you are not using the sights. Under stress, this is a natural reaction, but it is one you must train yourself to resist. Single, well-placed shots to the "T" of the zombie's eyes and nasal cavity are far more effective than a stream of bullets going every which way. Consider the future: with society in complete collapse, where are you going to get more ammunition? And will you have enough time to constantly reload magazines in the middle of a gunfight? Zombies will only die one at a time, so you should shoot them one at a time.

- *Consider Caliber:* The bigger the bullet, the big-

ger the hole. Rather than wasting shot after shot on one zombie that won't go down because the size of your rounds is insufficient to penetrate his skull, shoot it once with a large-caliber weapon and end the fight quickly. A headshot that doesn't blow its brains out won't significantly slow it down. Maximize your stopping power with as large a cartridge as you can put through the barrel.

- *Type of Cartridge:* With handguns, you have the choice of hollowpoint bullets or hardball. Hollowpoints have a small depression in the tip of the round that opens up the bullet on penetration, causing it to tumble, mushroom, and even fragment. The disadvantage of hollowpoints is that some calibers of them don't have the same skull-piercing power as hardball bullets. Hardball ammunition just punches right on through, deforming slightly less on impact. The drawback of hardball rounds is that they are more likely to shoot through the target and hit whatever or whomever is behind it. While there are no innocent bystanders in a fight against zombies, the chaos and movement inherent in combat may place one of your allies behind an undead target. Decide what the trade-off is worth and pick your ammo type accordingly.

Targets with Firearms

You can be the best shot in the world, but it won't save your life if you don't hit the right things. Whatever you're aiming at, make sure that you have a clear shot and you don't hesitate. There are no moral questions to be answered when killing zombies.

- *Head:* As with all weapons, this is the best target, bar none, for putting a zombie down permanently. The best place to hit on the head is the same as with a blade: the "T" of the eyes and nasal cavity. It is most likely that you will be shooting with a handgun in combat, as they are cheaper than carbines and more easily available, so proper targeting on the head is vital. A handgun bullet is much more likely to ricochet off the top of a skull than a rifle bullet. Shots to the temple are also effective, as the skull is thinner there. If shooting at a much taller zombie, firing

A headshot is the best choice when targeting the undead. (Illustration by Jennifer Larson.)

upward into its moaning mouth and through the soft palate into the brain also isn't a bad idea.

- *Neck:* Unless you shoot enough bullets to effect a decapitation, the neck isn't the best place to shoot on a zombie. You may get a good shot that hits the spinal column high enough to separate the head from the neck, but it's iffy.

- *Arms:* To do significant dismembering damage to an arm, you will need to put plenty of bullets into it. Rather than wasting shots to the arm, why not go for the head?

- *Torso:* An even worse target than the arm is the torso; shooting a zombie in the torso won't make much of a difference in its behavior unless you're able to completely bisect the trunk. Don't use up your ammo on shots to the body.

- *Legs:* Well-placed shots to the legs may do enough damage to the bones to cause the zombie to fall down, which is good. Remember, though, that you haven't killed it or stopped it from attacking you: all you've done is turned a walker into a crawler. Leg shots may be your only option if you don't have the time or marksmanship skills to get on the sights for a good headshot.

Specific Firearm Tactics

It might be that the only firearm you have is an old double-barreled twelve gauge that Granddad kept in the tool shed for shooting varmints, but it's still far, far better than having to hack at approaching zombies with a wood ax. Each firearm type has its own benefits, drawbacks, and effective zombie-killing tactics.

- *Revolver:* Some models of revolver can hold up to ten rounds, and a few of them have been designed to shoot shotgun shells. Just be aware that the recoil will be significant. Having at least two speedloaders is an absolute must when shooting with a revolver, as during the stress of combat it can be very difficult to load individual rounds into the cylinder. Unlike semiautomatics, revolvers cannot be silenced (Hollywood portrayals to the contrary), but as earlier stated, they are more reliable and jam less frequently. If your revolver goes "click" instead of "bang,"

just pull the trigger again. If it still refuses to fire and the cylinder won't swing open, you have a serious problem with your gun that cannot be fixed without a great deal of time and effort. This is rare, however; a quality revolver given regular maintenance is the most dependable firearm you can carry.

- *Semiautomatic:* The larger round capacity makes semiautomatics excellent weapons for dealing with multiple zombies at close range, but it also leaves them more susceptible to jamming at inopportune moments. If your semiautomatic goes "click" and doesn't indicate that it's empty by going to slide lock, perform a tap-rack-bang drill: turn your gun hand so that your palm is facing the sky, firmly hit (or "tap") the magazine at the bottom of the handle, turn your gun hand so the palm is facing the ground, rack the slide and let it go (*never* ride it forward with your hand), and get back to shooting. If this doesn't fix it, you have a dead gun for all intents and purposes, and probably won't have the time in a combat situation to effect a remedy. Transition to a secondary weapon (like a backup handgun).

- *Machine Gun:* To reiterate, with any automatic weapon it is important that you don't just spray lead everywhere. Just because your MP5 *can* unload 800 bullets per minute, it doesn't mean you should make it do so. They put the sights on there for a reason: use them, taking one shot at a time. Burst fire with a machine gun can be very effective, but be mindful that it eats up cartridges.

- *Shotgun:* Save the birdshot for shooting doves and skeet, and put either buckshot or slugs into your weapon. The farther your distance to the target, the wider the spread pattern. Don't forget, however, that at greater distances your shot begins to lose velocity and accuracy. You cannot take out two or three closely grouped zombies at a time with a load of buckshot at twenty yards: all you'll do is put holes in their faces and make them uglier. At close range you can start blowing limbs off, but you're still better off saving your rounds for the head. Shotgun slug rounds have excellent skull penetration no matter where on the head you hit, and you will rarely have to make a follow-up shot on the same target. Just have a mop ready for the brains and blood.

- *Assault Rifle:* Especially at medium to close range, a carbine can do zombie-killing damage with a minimum of shots. Stick with single shots, aim for the head, and you won't have to worry about ricochet: every round will go right through the skull.
- *Sniper Rifle:* You can kill zombies at truly epic distances with a good sniper rifle, but make sure that you have a close-range backup weapon that you can draw in a hurry in case you get snuck up on, like a revolver. Don't aim for the limb if you can hit the head: this isn't a game. Every zombie you kill is one less for someone else to deal with. A sniper rifle is employed when you have the time and space to plan your shots; don't expect to use it for every combat situation.

Such add-ons as laser or reflex sights, flashlight attachments, sidesaddles for shotgun shells, high-powered scopes, and other such devices can vastly enhance your combat effectiveness. What is more important, however, is that you practice shooting the weapon you're most comfortable with. Don't buy a shotgun, put all sorts of bells and whistles on it, and avoid going to the shooting range because the kick from the recoil bruises the hell out of your shoulder. The best weapon for you is the one you can work with to put life-ending holes into an enemy at a distance.

DEFENSES AGAINST ZOMBIE ATTACKS

You're can't always shoot your undead enemies from long range, especially if there are a lot of them closing fast. Get used to the idea that you are always going to be attacked when the circumstances are most unfavorable to you and optimum for your attacker. Zombies are just lucky that way, and if you are unfortunate enough to find yourself in a zombie apocalypse, you need to know how to avoid being killed by the walking dead. Do everything possible to put distance between you and the zombie, but be prepared to defend yourself properly if you have to go hand-to-hand. A proper defense will consist of three things: armor, agility, and tactics.

Armor

Not being hit is the best way to avoid being hurt. However, no one has a perfect all-around defense against being touched, so a necessary part of your personal protection will be a thicker outer layer—i.e., armor. Because human teeth aren't naturally very sharp, zombies are generally not strong enough to bite through metal or similar heavy, tough protection. Even a little armor, like a leather coat, is better than just a T-shirt. Be prepared to sacrifice a little mobility for that extra layer of life-saving protection.

- *Protect Your Extremities Above All Else:* Wearing gloves or gauntlets and bite-proof footwear is a no-brainer for the smart zombie killer. In combat, an unencumbered hand may flail around and get bitten by a hungry ghoul, and that one zombie you plugged in the kneecap and dropped can still crawl up to you fast enough to begin gnawing on your ankles while you're otherwise occupied. Cut the fingertips off the forefingers of your gloves so you can get a good tactile index on the trigger, and wear boots that protect your ankles at the very least. For head protection, a motorcycle helmet isn't a bad idea, but don't sacrifice too much of your peripheral vision. Favorite places for zombies to bite include the neck and shoulders, so a gorget (collar) and armored shoulder pads are very important. If nothing else, an extra layer of leather sewn into the shoulders of your jacket can be the all-important centimeter that keeps you uninfected. It's OK if they bruise you, but don't let them break the skin.
- *Don't Go Crazy:* It's impractical and uncomfortable, especially in the summer months, to wear a full set of armor all day every day, no matter how well constructed it is. Only armor the places you are most likely to be bitten: arms, hands, legs, feet, shoulders, neck, and face. Unless you're crowded on all sides by teeming hordes of the undead (in which case you are in really bad shape), you are probably not going to be subject to bites on the chest, stomach, or buttocks. Groin protection is optional, though for security's sake, it's probably better to wear some kind of cup.

Kevlar or chain mail provides excellent protection against zombie attacks. (Illustration by Martin Reimann.)

- *Kevlar:* Kevlar is an excellent source of protection from both the raking of zombie teeth and handgun rounds shot from a looter's .45. Most of the time, your Kevlar-buying options only extend to bulletproof vests, but these can be cut apart and resewn into any shape you require. Most army-navy stores sell Kevlar vests, and even those that have been decommissioned are still viable bite protection. Whatever you do, make sure that the seams are properly sealed. The last thing you want is for your suit of zombie-proof armor to get torn apart by the tugging of undead hands in your first combative outing.

- *Chain Mail Can Be Worn Outside of a Renaissance Faire:* Mail is the next best thing to Kevlar but can be difficult to find and even more difficult to make. A hauberk of mail consists of hundreds and hundreds of metal loops, all of which must be linked together by hand. The benefits to mail armor are manifold: you can fashion it into a perfectly fitting suit that only covers what you want to protect, it will resist even the strongest jaw of the hungriest zombie you can encounter, and it won't overly limit your combative movement. It can be heavy, but a reasonably fit person can get used to its weight in a matter of days. Mail does require some upkeep: occasional oiling to keep the links from getting too rusty, repair with pliers and substitute links due to the vicissitudes of combat, and regular refitting for when parts stretch or sag over time. Construction can be quite a chore, but the end result is relatively inexpensive and reliable.

Agility

Keep in mind that zombies want one thing—your brain—and the favored method of getting it is through biting. Teeth aren't the only weapons in the zombie arsenal, however. The undead will try to grab you and hold you down for that ravenous bite, so you have to be mobile to avoid their grasp. Don't dawdle because you think your armor protects you from bites; consider armor your last resort.

- *Stay Moving at All Times:* No matter what, you should always be on the move when engaged in close-quarters combat with the undead. Don't just stand there and try to duke it out with them one at a time, because they won't fight that way. They'll come at you en masse, and if they completely surround you, it's a matter of time before they pull you to the ground and find a place on you that their teeth can worry through. To keep from being crowded and surrounded, keep moving. Circle them and attack at angles to force them to chase you around. If they're chasing you, they're not eating you. Attack them from behind as much as possible. If you don't have the room to move, a good, hard shoulder strike to shove a zombie into its undead allies can open up a hole through which you can flee.

- *Speed Saves Lives:* Train to be quick. Part of winning a fight is attacking where your opponent is weak and exploiting his shortcomings to your advantage. Zombies are slow and clumsy, so work at becoming fast and agile. The only way to become quick is to train at it through exercise and constant drilling. Build fast-twitch muscle fiber through plyometric calisthenics and the flow drills taught in this text. If you wait for an emergency before you decide to get off the couch and into the gym, your chances for survival plummet.

- *Blocking:* Every block of a zombie's attack should be a strike of some kind, and every combat movement should either take you farther away from the enemy or significantly damage him. Whenever an undead hand grabs for you, hack it off. To bite you, a zombie must bring its decaying face close, which is a perfect opportunity for a thrust into the eye or a punch in the teeth with a mailed gauntlet. Imagine yourself as a Cuisinart food processor, chopping, slicing, shooting, and destroying anything that gets within reach. The best defense is killing all your enemies before they can kill you.

Tactics

Zombies, by their very nature, are unintelligent, so it shouldn't be terribly difficult to outsmart them. Their single-mindedness is a two-edged sword: they will stop at nothing to get you, but that makes them very easy to fool. The zombie solution to every problem is a straight-line attack. While they lack the wherewithal to avoid most traps, they won't always just run off a cliff or jump into a grain thresher for you. Zombie dumb luck cannot be overestimated, and Murphy's Law oversees all combat operations.

- *Tricks and Traps:* Zombies will simply go at anything they see as food without heed for the consequences, so they are easily led into ambushes. A deep pit covered by leaves with human bait beyond it can trap any number of hungry undead, for example. Leading zombies into a building rigged with explosives, causing them to walk among tripwire-activated shotguns set up at head height, or just dropping heavy objects on them from the top of a building are other examples. Blunderers that they are, zombies will fall for just about any trick, trap, or snare you set. Circumstance, assets, and your particular situation will inform your tactics.
- *Avoidance:* There is great benefit to running away so you can live to fight another day. You don't *have* to kill every zombie you see, especially if the noise of combat will attract other walking dead who happen to be nearby. Through bad luck or unfortunate circumstance, every fight can be your last, so choose your battles carefully. Avoid unnecessary conflicts.
- *Stack Them Up:* You will most likely be fighting multiple opponents, but it doesn't necessarily mean that you will have to fight them all at the same time. Use your movement and agility to stack your undead assailants, causing them to blunder into each other in their haste to get at you. This also means that you must never let yourself be cornered. Fleeing is fine, whether it is to put yourself in a better position to counterattack or leave the danger zone entirely. Never enter an area that only has one exit.

THE ZOMBIE-KILLING MINDSET

The "at all costs" survival mentality you must cultivate as a survivor of the zombie apocalypse extends also to those occasions in which you have to use violence to end the horrible unlife granted to the walking dead. Violence is unspeakably ugly and rough and will never go as you plan, especially when you are fighting zombies. Some things to take into account when developing the zombie-killing mindset include:

- *Mercy Is for the Weak:* Because zombies ask for no quarter, you must give them none. Mercy is an irrelevant concept to a monster whose only purpose is to eat your brain and who will stop at nothing to get it. Just as you have your own "at all costs" mindset, so does the zombie. Even if the zombie you are fighting was once a very close loved one, holding back now will only ensure your demise. Every ghoul you kill is one less creature that will terrorize and murder another innocent victim, so don't get wrapped up in moral questions of pity and compassion. Become merciless in your dealings with the undead, as they themselves will give you no clemency.
- *Why Ask Why?:* Don't get wrapped up in such questions as why the zombies are doing what they're doing, why this is happening to the world, or why you are in this very struggle right now. Such thoughts are dangerous distractions and take your mental focus away from your immediate survival concerns. Asking why all the time is just another example of your becoming a spectator in your life instead of actually living it. Leave that to the philosophers that your fight will pave the way for in future generations. If you are going to fight to defend yourself and your very species, don't concern yourself with anything else. Distraction kills.
- *The Power of Will:* A strong stomach and an indomitable fighting spirit count more in a fight than all the zombie combat drills ever practiced. It is no easy thing to take up a machete and hack at the neck of a gibbering, drooling, stinking, undead thing that used to be a man, and if you have never mentally prepared yourself for the task, you might freeze or flail wildly at the moment of truth. Get used to the stink of dead blood and decaying flesh, the sight of exposed viscera and necrotic tissue, the feel of cold hands and raking nails. It's perfectly OK to experience fear, but if you let it dominate and

control you, then you are as good as dead, or worse. A cool head and a laser-like focus on victory will do wonders for your survivability in the zombie apocalypse.

FIGHTING SPECIFIC ZOMBIE TYPES

The techniques described in previous sections are applicable to just about any sort of zombie you're likely to face in a combat situation. Even so, you may want to adjust your tactics a little, depending on the specific type of zombie you're up against. The 24-hour news cycle we live in is an advantage in that a zombie apocalypse initiated by the Gates of Hell literally opening up in the middle of Times Square will be widely reported, with pictures and video. The same goes for a virally caused zombie uprising getting out of control and becoming an epidemic, and so on. Unless you are unfortunate enough to be at Zombie Ground Zero when the undead begin to rise, the kind of zombies you will be facing probably won't be a complete mystery: the media will describe them to you before you are forced to do battle.

Viral Zombie Tactics

Viral zombies are usually physically stronger than supernatural zombies, mostly because of how quickly the zombie-causing pathogen can kill the infected. This means that these zombies are, for lack of a better term, "fresher" and more likely to have greater muscle mass and bodily integrity. The animating principle behind them is biologically based and hence *may* follow more traditional rules of how the body can behave.

- *They Are Always Hungry:* Viral zombies are hungrier for brains and human flesh than any other zombie type. It has been theorized that this undead state causes them great physical agony, which can only be temporarily mitigated by the consumption of human brain matter. Head, neck, and shoulder protection is absolutely necessary when fighting this kind of zombie, from a motorcycle helmet or mail coif to an armored collar and bite-resistant shoulder pads. Just as your attacks should always go to the

head, their attacks will do likewise.

- *Their Bite Is Worse Than Their Bark:* Biting is the viral zombie's primary form of attack, followed by grabbing you to keep you immobile for the bite. They won't deliberately kick or punch or stomp you, and they won't let up their attack until they've eaten your brain. Whatever they can reach, they'll bite. Knocking their teeth out is only a delaying tactic: if their virus-ridden blood or saliva gets into an open wound anywhere on your body, it's only a matter of time before you become one of their number.

- *There May Be Runners:* Because of their relative freshness, viral zombies are more likely to be able to run after you at living human speeds. This can present a significant problem, especially if you're trying to flee from them with full gear on. Their speed doesn't make them any less clumsy, and in their ungainly haste they will be subject to falling down or up staircases, tripping over obstacles, or blundering into planned ambushes. They do not get tired, however, and lactic acid buildup won't slow them down. The only good news is that, when rot starts to set into their muscles, running zombies will eventually become walking and shuffling zombies.

- *Fresh Zombies Are Sturdy Zombies:* Because decay hasn't significantly rotted away its body, a recently turned zombie will be a stronger and tougher adversary than a zombie created weeks ago. As such, a fresh zombie will be harder to defeat in hand-to-hand combat, though it can still be killed with relative ease by a well-placed bullet. Involuntary muscular tension and a relatively hardy skeleton will make the viral zombie more difficult to decapitate or dismember, but the "T" of the eyes and nose is still an excellent place for a death-dealing sword thrust. Be aware that you may have to hack harder and more often at the neck to get that undead head to come off.

- *Viral Zombies Will Be Everywhere:* There will be far more of them than there are of you. If the merest bite or other transference of bodily fluids from zombie to person can infect the living, imagine how many zombies there will be once the outbreak has become too much for the government to handle. The unfortunates who

A zombie's bite is much worse than his bark. (Illustration by Jennifer Larson.)

escaped a zombie's grasp after being bitten will soon turn into undead themselves, and they'll infect others who will in turn infect yet others, and on and on and on. That scenario only accounts for the living who were infected by the zombie threat. What if this pathogen also infects the long-dead? Prepare yourself to be always outnumbered, with every fight against multiple undead opponents. Maintain the principles of mobility and avoidance and flee as fast as you can to the least populated area you can reach.

Supernatural Zombie Tactics

The good news is that supernatural zombies don't usually propagate their own kind through biting, so if you're bitten, you won't necessarily become a slavering undead fiend in a few days or hours. The bad news is that when the veil between life and death has been ripped away, each and every dead person on the planet can be raised up to harrow the living. In this event, it is likely that many of the undead you will face will be more rotten (and hence "softer") than viral zombies: some may have been dead for quite some time before rising from the grave. The uniquely appalling thing about a supernatural zombie apocalypse is that you can no longer trust any of the rules of physics—they've all gone out the window, and what you once believed, what you once *knew* was or wasn't possible, is now a lie.

- *Detached Limbs Have a Life of Their Own:* If you dismember a supernatural zombie, its detached limbs may still be capable of attacking you. This may not be much of a problem if it's a hacked-off leg, but a collection of animate hands and arms can still grab you or otherwise hamper your movements. This becomes particularly troubling if you cut off a supernatural zombie's head and the rest of it just keeps coming after you. Even though it may be immediately easier to combatively dissect a softer, more rotten supernatural zombie, avoid the temptation and instead stab or shoot its brain.
- *Stay Away from the Cemetery:* A supernatural zombie apocalypse will be heralded by the dead literally rising from the grave, so the most dan-

gerous place to be when the trouble starts is a cemetery. Consider this, however: many cemeteries these days insist on the use of a burial vault, which is a container made of metal, hard plastic, or concrete into which the coffin is sealed. This protects the casket from moisture and the settling weight of the earth on top of it. It would be monumentally difficult for even the most motivated zombie to break out of a coffin, burst through its burial vault, dig its way up through six feet of dirt, and still be in any condition to effectively attack the living. Despite that, burial vaults are not required everywhere, so you should still stay as far away from graveyards as possible.

- *Bodily Condition:* Supernatural zombies can range from newly risen corpses full of vigor to moldering half-skeletons bearing a small clot of putrefying brown glop where its brain used to be. Even a decayed zombie from the nineteenth century can still be a formidable opponent, especially in a group. Don't underestimate the strength an even decades-long-undead corpse can muster, and treat every fight as if it were your last.
- *Who Is the Master?:* Unlike viral zombies, supernatural zombies don't just occur by accident. Someone or some*thing* deliberately raised the dead, and who or whatever it is, it does not have your best interests at heart. Supernatural zombies were raised for a reason, usually simple destruction, mayhem, and murder. If you should happen to see the sorcerer, vampire, or demon responsible for calling up the dead to plague the living—run. Avoid the Master at all costs.

Voodoo Zombie Tactics

As previously stated, a voodoo zombie apocalypse is a less likely scenario than a viral zombie apocalypse. Nevertheless, it is important to recognize the danger a voodoo zombie can pose and prepare for the worst. The information presented here can turn the tide and keep a zombie uprising from becoming a full-blown zombie apocalypse.

- *There Will Be Blood:* Voodoo zombies aren't necessarily undead creatures but rather living humans possessed by evil spirits, black magic, or powerful drugs. While essentially mindless, they are still alive and subject to most of the same rules as other living beings. As such, they can die through blood loss or vital organ failure. A cut to the neck can be deadly to a voodoo zombie, even if you don't sever the head. It will just take some time. Killing a voodoo zombie is thus not entirely unlike killing a living human being. Just keep in mind that it can get messy and horrible in a way killing an undead, unfeeling creature can't.

- *What's My Motivation?:* Though not always cannibalistic, voodoo zombies have a reason for doing what they do and being what they are. This reason might not be immediately apparent, but remember that it is not smart to ask why in the extremis of a combat situation. When you come up on a voodoo zombie, don't ask any questions. Just kill it.
- *Weapon vs. Weapon:* In rare cases, you might face a voodoo zombie armed with a weapon like a knife or a club. Always deal with the immediate threat first: cut the arm holding the weapon until it or the limb is gone; then go about the bloody business of finishing off the rest of the creature. A thrust to the belly with a rusty knife wielded by a voodoo zombie is almost always a fatal wound when monsters have over-run all the hospitals.
- *Give Me Just a Little More Time:* The spell or drug that animates the voodoo zombie may wear off over time, whereas a truly undead state lasts forever. It may be that a voodoo zombie apocalypse causes all of its civilization-destroying damage in its first few months before subsiding. This may be good for humanity in the long run, but when it comes to your immediate survival, it doesn't matter. A zombie is a zombie, and a fight is a fight. Deal with each day as it comes, and don't lower your guard until the very last zombie on the planet is down for the count.

Survival in the ZOMBIE Apocalypse

Human beings have an amazing ability to adapt to the most adverse conditions, and what is an unlivable wilderness to some may be a cornucopia of resources to others. One need only look at the shantytown of Bihar in India, Garbage City in Egypt, or the Kalahari Bush in southern Africa to see that we as a species are incredibly tough and resilient. The inhabitants of these harsh environments survive through adaptation, ingenuity, and the indomitability of the human spirit. If primitive people can survive millennia of desert living by eating insects for nourishment and getting their water from wild-grown melons, you can get by for a few years in a zombie-ravaged America. It just takes skill and perseverance.

The importance of so-called "primitive skills" cannot be overstated, and the time to begin acquiring and practicing them is now. Hunting, fishing, identifying potable water, and building shelter in difficult conditions require knowledge to do well. When the unquiet dead rise up to destroy civilization, you will not automatically know how to do these things properly. Trial and error is for laboratory experiments, not survival situations. It's your life: do you want to be a driver or a passenger?

We have already discussed that the most important thing in a zombie apocalypse is keeping your-self from becoming dead or undead. Everything else is secondary. This chapter deals with those secondary concerns, which we will call Problem B. Problem A is just getting through the day without getting your brains eaten by zombies. Problem B is acquiring food and water, finding shelter or constructing a zombie redoubt, determining the best allies and associates to help you survive, and identifying the characteristics of a good vehicle to drive when zombies have taken over. For what is probably the first time in your life, your survival is entirely in *your* hands. Take hold.

FOOD AND WATER ACQUISITION

When zombies have taken over the Earth, the concept of private ownership, especially of relatively small things like food items, goes completely out the window. That is, it's no longer theft when it's the end of the world. If you are unable to hunt for your food because of your locale, skill set, or circumstances, then you must scavenge for it. In an apocalyptic survival situation, there is no stigma or shame attached to scavenging: your life in a world of plenty was taken from you by teeming hordes of undead. While scavenging might be as easy as breaking into the local convenience store and grabbing all the beef

During a zombie apocalypse the only law is the law of the jungle. You will have to compete with everyone else for the limited resources available. (Illustration by Jennifer Larson.)

jerky left on the shelf, there are some factors to keep in mind that will increase your survivability.

Competing for Resources

You will probably not be the last human left on Earth when zombies have destroyed civilization and eaten the brains of everyone you ever loved. You will not only have to fight for your life, but you will also have to fight for sustenance, as well. Everyone else

who hasn't been turned into the walking dead has to eat, too, and those who survive the first few dangerous weeks of the zombie apocalypse are likely to be very tough customers, indeed. Remember that the only law is the law of the jungle. When dealing with your fellow scavengers, consider the following:

- *It's You or Him:* Not to put too fine a point on it, but you just may have to kill your neighbor for that last can of pork and beans. This is not to say that you should survive by taking food from other living humans, but you must realize that they might try to take what's yours, and they'll do so by stealth or force. Make a list of every person you know who would die for you if they had to. Everyone else not on that list would, if hungry and frightened enough, do anything and everything necessary to ensure his own survival.

- *Compassion within Limits:* Once you set up your zombie redoubt and develop a solid plan for your defense and provisioning during the zombie apocalypse, you will be tempted to include your friends and neighbors. It's only natural to want to help other human beings. *Don't do it.* Your primary responsibility is to yourself and your family. You can't feed everybody. If your survival through a long and hungry winter comes down to your family of ants not sharing your grain with the grasshoppers next door, then there really is no choice at all. Gratitude and empathy are only feelings, and all feelings are temporary. Harden your heart and focus on your own survival before all others.

- *Bandits and You:* The preceding paragraphs will seem unduly harsh to anyone who has not had to directly and personally confront the issues a zombie apocalypse presents. It is a hard and selfish heart that will see you through, not the warm feelings of community and sharing. This does not mean, however, that you should become a thief and murderer, nor does it mean that your merciless attitude toward the undead should extend to every last living person. If you survive the zombie apocalypse and lose your own soul in the process, you have done half the zombies' work for them. Unfortunately, it is likely that many surviving humans will themselves turn to robbery and murder to get provisions during the zombie apocalypse and become bandits. As more cunning adversaries than the average zombie, they will present another danger you will have to deal with. You will not be able to find common ground with people who have decided they have nothing left to lose, so do not try. Bandits

have divorced themselves from everything that is ethical and worth saving, so no matter what their justification, treat them as you would a zombie coming after your brains.

Food

The epidemic of obesity in many industrialized nations has taught us one thing: modern human beings do not know how to eat properly. We have almost completely separated ourselves from the knowledge of where, exactly, our food comes from, what we should be eating, and what it takes to bring our food to the dinner table. If you haven't figured out how to stay nourished and healthy *before* the zombie apocalypse, you will be in for an extremely unpleasant surprise when the graveyards begin vomiting forth hostile, ambulatory corpses.

Survival situations are often about just making do with what you can, so you need to retrain your food preferences. Veganism is a luxury only the wealthy can afford. Peking duck won't be available when all the chefs have been turned into zombies. Our culture of celebrity chefs, cooking-based television networks, and cheap fast food on every corner is unsustainable *now* for long-term species survival, let alone the zombie apocalypse. The walking dead only have one food choice: your brains, and they will get them raw.

Don't think that you absolutely *must* have three hot meals a day to get by. Just because you're hungry, it doesn't mean that you have to eat immediately. Depending on your physical condition and level of activity, you can get by for a month or even more without eating, though it isn't recommended. Part of your training to survive the zombie apocalypse is learning the difference between hunger and actual starvation, when your body begins to break down from lack of nourishment. When acquiring food under these apocalyptic conditions, consider the following:

- *Cans:* Canned food is a lifesaver, but it will not last forever. Most canned meats, fruits, and vegetables will last at least two years and perhaps much longer. The shelf life of a can containing higher-acid foods, such as tomatoes or citrus fruit, is two years maximum. Dented cans are

OK to eat from, but never eat anything from a can that is leaking or otherwise pierced in some way when you found it. Likewise if the can is bulging from one or both ends, this means that its contents are spoiled and have begun to decay. Canned food can be heavy, so if you lead a nomadic lifestyle, it will be challenging to tote around a long-term food supply. Whatever you do, no matter how hungry you are, do *not* eat canned dog food. Canned dog food may contain bone meal and other ingredients harmful to the human digestive system. Cat food is slightly more acceptable to eat.

- *Junk:* Packaged junk food doesn't usually have the nutrients necessary to keep you healthy and vigorous during the zombie apocalypse, but it does last long in the wrapper and can be valuable for trade purposes. A consequence of living in the twenty-first century is the ubiquity of junk food, so it shouldn't be hard to find. An emergency supply of candy bars and cheese crackers can, if rationed properly, lift the spirits and provide a temporary energy boost. Just remember that you can't live on junk food forever.

- *Spoiled Rotten:* If you get hungry enough, it may become very tempting to eat spoiled or otherwise rotten food. This is a mistake. It's difficult enough for your body to function when it is truly famished, but it's even harder if you force it to deal with food poisoning or botulism on top of the weakness that starvation brings. Be aware that everything starts to look good when you're really hungry, but resist the temptation to do something harmful in the moment. If it smells bad or is otherwise questionable, don't eat it. Zombies find hungry living brains just as tasty as sated living brains, and they will find it easier to get them from your head when you're doubled over from the Hershey squirts from gobbling down a gone-over pack of hot dogs found in an abandoned butcher shop.

- *Nutrition and You:* A comprehensive discussion on proper nutrition is beyond the scope of this text, but a good rule of thumb is if you practice a diet that you read about in a best-selling book, you're probably not doing much good for yourself. Fad diets are just that: fads. Don't put your

life in a celebrity nutritionist's hands. The U.S. Government's Food Pyramid is a sham, so throw that out as well. Simply get a good balance of carbohydrates, proteins, and fats, and listen to your body. When it needs something, it will tell you. Between vitamin supplements found in stores (Vitamin C is a must-have) and whatever you can hunt for, scavenge, or forage, you can stay relatively healthy and nourished between zombie attacks.

- *Foraging:* Urban foraging has become a fad of late, which is both a good and a bad thing. It's good because there is now a wealth of information available on which plants and animals in your locale are edible and nutritious. Unfortunately, it is also bad *because* of the availability of this information. Instead of fighting for that last can of creamed corn, you may instead find that your favorite place to find edible cattails and plump rabbits has been overrun by your fellow hungry human beings. Learn what is good to eat and, more importantly, what *isn't* good to eat near your zombie redoubt to enhance your diet of canned food and MREs.

- *Go to the Shops:* Obviously, the best places to find ready-made food are grocery stores, supermarkets, convenience stores, restaurants, shopping malls, and department stores. America's obesity epidemic can be a benefit to the hungry traveler, in that just about every office building, business, or government structure has some kind of food stored or hidden away. You just have to find it. If there are no such buildings nearby, you may have to resort to breaking into private homes and residences to find nourishment. Be aware that zombies and bandits may be lurking in any of these places, and stay alert at all times.

- *Stop All This Cannibalism: Never* resort to cannibalism of any kind, no matter how famished you are. In addition to this act turning you into a living zombie, of sorts, the taste for human flesh has been long considered addictive. On top of that, consuming human brain matter puts you at significant risk of contracting kuru, a degenerative neurological disease that causes body tremors, headaches, insanity, and death. Boil your belt and shoes to make leather soup if you

The best places to find ready-made food are grocery stores and supermarkets, but they may be mobbed by the undead. (Illustration by Martin Reimann.)

have to, but don't eat your fellow man. It shouldn't have to be said that eating a zombie, even a deanimated one, is probably the worst thing you could possibly do.

Water

You can go a month or more without food, but you won't last more than a few days without water. Despite today's hysteria about personal hydration, most of us get much of our body's water requirements through the food we eat. It's common knowledge that if you feel thirsty, you're already dehydrated, but a little dehydration isn't going to kill you. Learn to tell the difference between the mild dis-

comfort of thirst and the physical debilitation of true dehydration so that you will have a better idea of how to marshal your water resources properly. Everyone's water needs will differ according to body type, climate, geography, and level of activity, so there are only a few hard and fast rules about water in the zombie apocalypse.

- *Salt Talks:* Hacking and shooting at zombies are very taxing activities, day or night. Combat is the most stressful thing you will have to deal with during the Zombie End Times. Stress makes you sweat, and as you perspire and lose your body's water, you will also start to lose

You won't last more than a day without a source of fresh water. Whatever you do, don't drink water from any ponds, which may contain deadly pathogens. (Illustration by Jennifer Larson.)

salt. Symptoms of salt loss include fainting, vomiting, lower blood pressure, and exhaustion. While it's not a good idea to eat a lot of salty foods, such as potato chips, when your water supply is low, remember to take salt tablets if you do a lot of sweating.

• *Locate Natural Water Sources:* When the municipal water supply stops pumping, you will no longer be able to depend on the faucet to provide hydration unless you have a well or private aquifer. Now is the time to scout out and locate other sources of water, *before* this becomes a problem. Streams, creeks, rivers, lakes, reservoirs, and ponds: map out where they are and calculate how long it will take to get to them on foot from your zombie redoubt. This beats having to dodge the walking dead while on a blind search for something to drink.

• *The Bottled Stuff:* Bottled water is an excellent, if limited, source of hydration. Commercially sealed bottled water has, for all intents and purposes, an indefinite shelf life. It may taste a little funny after years, but it won't be harmful if unopened. One caveat is that you should not treat the local supermarket as your regular private watering hole. Carry as much water as you can back to your zombie redoubt and then go back for seconds and thirds. You can ration it at home. The more often you make regular trips to where other people can find water, the more likely it is that you'll become the victim of bandits. Because bottled water is immediately potable, unlike standing water, don't waste it for cleaning purposes. Better to be a little smelly and hydrated than clean and thirsty.

• *Personal Hygiene:* Societal pressure on human beings to be clean and sweet-smelling at all times has created an overreliance on the frequent use of otherwise potable water as a cleaning agent. The bottom line is that we waste a lot of water keeping ourselves clean. If you want to survive the zombie apocalypse, you will have to break this self-imposed requirement of daily washing. This is not to say that you should live as a dirty, unkempt savage, but get comfortable with the idea of somewhat looser hygiene habits. A bath in that stream a mile from your

house may be tempting, but if you saw a band of shuffling undead cross through it earlier, it's still a risk not worth taking. One thing that should *not* go by the wayside is proper dental care, however. Poor nutrition can loosen your teeth, which is bad enough. When zombies have destroyed civilization, it's a strong likelihood that your dentist is no longer keeping regular office hours, if at all. Brush and floss regularly.

• *Water Purification:* Don't immediately trust water that hasn't been commercially bottled. Standing water is potentially harmful on its own, and even running water from rivers and streams can contain pathogens that are dangerous to living human beings. Water filtration bottles, while expensive, are excellent investments. Follow the directions for use and acquire extra filters, and you won't have to worry about finding bottled water again. Failing that, commercially available iodine tablets will purify water, as will boiling it for a few minutes. The only concern about purifying found water is that if you are in the unfortunate position of having to survive a viral zombie apocalypse, the virus/chemical or nanites that created the zombies may be heat-, filter-, or iodine-resistant. In that case, avoid any water source that zombies have traveled through as though your life depended on it. No matter how skilled a zombie killer you become, you can still be felled by a waterborne zombie virus and not know it until you develop a ravenous hunger for gray matter.

MEDICINE

Spare no expense when it comes to getting a fully stocked first aid kit, and make sure that you know how to use what's in it. Accidents can happen to anyone, and what started out as a small cut from a car antenna or a scratch from stumbling down a broken staircase can turn into a staph infection or worse without proper care. The only cure for a zombie bite is a bullet to the brain, but be prepared for other medical contingencies so you won't be caught short in an emergency.

• *Prescription for Health:* There won't be time for

you to get mail-in refills on your prescription medication when the Emergency Broadcast System announces that cannibalistic undead are roaming the streets, so keep at least an extra month's supply near you at all times. Ration it out to make it last as long as possible, and do a harsh self-examination to determine if you really need it. Valium, Viagra, and the like are drugs you can probably get by without for the time being, as most of your mental processes will be focused on not being killed by zombies. Statin drugs and antidepressants are also likely to be less important than aspirin and antibiotics. Prioritize your drug requirements, and you'll be surprised at what you can survive without.

- *Antibiotics:* The misuse of antibiotics in today's industrialized nations has created some very drug-resistant superbugs. Remember that antibiotics are only good for treating bacterial and some fungal infections, and won't do any good against viruses (especially zombie-creating viruses). Still, it's better to have some than not. Certain countries like Mexico have made some antibiotics easier to get without a doctor's prescription, so stock up now. The rule is that if you begin taking an antibiotic for an infection, make sure you take it according to medical recommendations, even if you stop showing symptoms and have some pills left.
- *Painkillers:* Such over-the-counter pain relievers as aspirin, ibuprofen, and acetaminophen are must-haves in any medical kit, but it's not a bad idea to acquire something stronger in case you should be subject to a painful injury like a broken bone. Many such drugs are available online without a prescription, but be aware that in some cases you may be purchasing a formed and painted nugget of building material in place of the actual drug. Test before an emergency.
- *Go to the Vet:* The medications, antibiotics, and painkillers prescribed for pets are, in most cases, chemically identical to the drugs we humans take for similar ailments. In many cases, the dog or cat versions of these drugs are easier to obtain. While I cannot and will not encourage illegal activity in this text, it might be suggested that you independently study what prescription drugs treat what disorders, such as infection, pain relief, and internal sicknesses. From there, an unscrupulous person might bring his pet to the vet and claim that his animal is showing symptoms consistent with these ailments. As the dog or cat isn't capable of verbally denying the claim, a sympathetic vet might prescribe with few questions asked. Legal concerns force me to state that you should not do this under any circumstances. Ever.
- *Pop Down to the Chemist:* The highest security at any shop, save for jewelers' and check-cashing establishments, is at the local pharmacy. This is not to say that a determined and resourceful individual cannot break into one, but it will be far more difficult to do so than shooting through a supermarket window to grab a box of Band-Aids. If you are in an emergency situation and need pharmacy-grade medication fast, trying to break into a drugstore may not be your best option. You might be fortunate enough to find an unlooted pharmacy or hospital whose employees were killed by the walking dead before they could lock up, but it is not an opportunity to be depended upon.

SHELTER

The benefits of a nomadic lifestyle are far outweighed by the advantages of living in a shelter that you can sleep safely in, defend from outside attack, and use as a storage place for supplies. It is a truly miserable feeling to be out in the elements without a safe haven you can call your own, especially when the walking dead are stumbling behind you with outstretched arms. The oft-touted romanticism of traveling the highways without roots or cares starts to fade after the first long winter night spent shivering in the vestibule of an office building you couldn't break into.

The Zombie Redoubt

A zombie redoubt is a fort, your first line of defense from zombie attack. If you are fortunate enough to have the means to purchase or construct a purpose-designed structure to keep you safe from

Living in a tent is not a good idea during a zombie apocalypse. Find safe shelter that you can defend from attack by both the dead and undead. (Illustration by Rolf Harding.)

both the elements and the grasping hands of hungry zombies, then you will find the information here valuable. If you lack such resources, you can still learn a great deal from this section and adapt your current living arrangements so that no matter where you hang your hat, you can still mount a proper defense and live in relative comfort.

A zombie redoubt has a set of characteristics that separate it from an ordinary home or other living space, specific to the demands of living in a world where the undead have destroyed civilization. These characteristics include:

- *Invisibility:* Don't be the only house on the block with bars on the windows and high-tech electronic locks on the exterior doors. This tells zombies, bandits, and intrusive government functionaries that something good and worth taking is inside. Drawing attention to yourself with a highly visible security profile is asking for trouble in a high-risk situation, including a zombie apocalypse. If you must board up your windows, for example, build a predesigned frame that you can nail into the studs of your house from the *inside* when the undead roam the streets.

- *Impregnability:* Your zombie redoubt must be easily defended from outside forces. Zombies, while barely sentient, will still try to enter a structure through the doors or windows, so every portal to your home must be strengthened to withstand the shock of undead fists. For doors, this means steel doorframe reinforcements and impact-resistant deadbolts. Windows should have internally mounted security shutters and reinforced panes.

- *Surveillance:* Unobtrusively mounted security cameras both inside and outside the structure are good to have but will stop working when the power grid craps out. Go low-tech and place decorative mirrors near stairwells, corners, and hallways so you can see what's going on around you without having to give up a good fighting position. Make sure that any trees or shrubs you have planted outside don't block your view of what's going on in the street. You won't need an early-warning alarm system when dealing with approaching zombies: they don't move with care or stealth.

- *A Way to Escape:* Every room in your zombie redoubt that you spend any length of time in should have no less than two avenues of escape. Put rope ladders by the windows of your upper floors so you can make a quick getaway if you get surprised or cornered by zombies climbing the stairs. Don't use a windowless basement or cellar as the place where you'll make your last stand: you're guaranteeing that you won't get out of it.

- *A Weapon in Every Room:* No matter what else you do to improve your zombie redoubt's security, having a zombie-killing weapon in every room is a must. Don't rely on improvising if you don't have to. A heavy "antique" saber on the wall in the front room is a better choice than having to grab a paring knife from the kitchen on the fly. That curio cabinet in the family room should have a loaded pistol somewhere in it (made safe from the curious fingers of children, of course). And you should be able to hold off a small army of hungry zombies from just the arsenal in your bedroom, which is the place you are most likely to be caught unawares. Your comfort level with sharp things and devices that shoot lead will increase the more you practice with them, so having weapons nearby should not be a significant concern.

- *A Big Pantry:* The average man needs approximately 2,400–3,000 calories a day to function at physical peak. For women, it is a little less: 2,000–2,400 calories a day. These totals change according to age and the amount of regular physical activity you engage in: a fit young man needs more calories than an older, sedentary person, for example. You should have a three- to six-month supply of food in your pantry to get you through the critical first weeks of a zombie apocalypse, when things are at their most chaotic. If you live in a colder northern climate, you will probably want to store more food to keep from having to struggle through difficult weather conditions to find needed sustenance. This food supply can take many forms, from cans and dried food to military MREs. Make sure that your pantry has food that you actually *want* to eat: it's bad enough to have to fight zombies during the apocalypse, but it's much worse if you don't have a good dinner to come home to.

- *Water Supply:* The average person should drink about two liters of water a day, though this will vary according to physical activity, body size, age, and climate. If you perspire more, you should drink more. Always keep at least two months' more water than you think you will need. Remember that bottled water is relatively inexpensive and doesn't go bad in the package, but don't start using it until the municipal water supply goes out. Ration your water supply carefully and wisely, but don't put yourself into a state of dehydration if you don't have to.

- *A Hiding Place:* Every zombie redoubt should have at least one hiding place large enough to conceal yourself and, if necessary, one or two others. If you are in the unenviable position of having to provide for the safety and security of a spouse and small children during the zombie apocalypse, make sure that you have enough hiding places for them, as well. This hiding place is not intended to hide you from zombies, however: if a zombie thinks you are in a structure, it will never leave until it has been killed or has eaten your brain. Instead, there will be situations in which you will want to hide from your fellow humans: concealing yourself from roving bandits or military personnel seeking to take you to a detention camp, for example. The back of the closet is *not* a good hiding place, nor is under the bed. Better hiding places include a hollowed-out sofa, a purpose-built secret room behind a bookshelf, an old cabinet with a fake drawer façade, or a concealed crawlspace in the basement of your home. Be aware that while you're hiding, you can't do anything else, such as scan your area for threats or adequately defend yourself from attack.

- *The Zombie Safe Room:* Defending an entire home from rampaging zombies is difficult but doable under ideal circumstances. You might have to retreat within your home, however, to a more easily defended spot to regroup or plan an escape. This is your zombie safe room: a redoubt within your redoubt. The best place for a zombie safe room is the master bedroom of

your house. That way, if you are awakened or otherwise surprised in the night by the undead somehow breaking through the front door, you will already be in an ideal spot for defense. To make any interior room a zombie safe room, replace the hollow-core interior door with a lockable, steel-reinforced, solid-core exterior door (you may have to cut the door to size for it to fit within the frame); put at least a week's supply of food and water in the closet; have plenty of weapons and ammunition handy; and have a back way out, such as the rope ladder described earlier. Even if you don't have a good hiding place, can't afford enough weapons to place liberally around the home, and are unable to properly stock your pantry, at least set up a zombie safe room as your last line of defense.

Zombie-Proof Your Home

Some of you may live in apartments or condominiums, or be looking for a cheaper, more convenient way of turning your home into a zombie redoubt. Do not cut corners when it comes to your safety. Eat out less and dine in more, go to the movies less frequently and read books from the library, shop at Wal-Mart instead of Bloomingdales. Rather than buying that expensive watch that really *looks* good, focus on reliability and functionality, which never go out of style. When the armies of the soulless, cannibalistic undead begin shuffling across the face of the Earth looking for brains to eat, the brand of clothes you wear and the model of cell phone you carry become utterly meaningless. Personal security is, by its very nature, inconvenient. But it is far better than the alternative. Put yourself in the zombie-killing, apocalypse-surviving mindset, and in time you will magically be able to afford a few security upgrades.

- *Focus on the Front Door:* For you apartment dwellers who cannot or will not reinforce your front door with metal jamb protectors, shatter-proof deadbolts, and steel banding along the door frame, at the very least you should install a door security bar. Door security bars are removable, inexpensive, and will delay the undead for those vital few minutes while you escape or prepare a defense. In most cases, the door will need to be completely shattered before the door security bar will give.

- *Don't Forget the Windows:* Internally installed metal shutters are the best way to keep zombies from coming in through the windows, but you might not be able to afford it. In that case, your next best option is to have security window film professionally installed on all your first- and second-floor window glass. This overlay will not prevent the undead from breaking in, but like the door security bar, it will significantly slow them down. Failing that, put together premeasured wooden frames with boards nailed across that can be hammered or screwed into the wall when trouble starts. Store them out of the way (but instantly accessible) until they become necessary.

- *Those Nice Glass Doors:* Aside from sliding patio doors, French doors are probably the worst things you could have in a home you want to protect from zombies. Have them replaced with sturdy solid-core doors as soon as possible. If you cannot do this for whatever reason, have the glass reinforced with security film and just be prepared to retreat to your zombie safe room the moment you hear the first zombie hit the pane.

- *No Home Is Forever:* No matter how much time, effort, and money you have invested in your zombie redoubt, be prepared to leave it if you have to. Don't try to defend a position that has been overrun, no matter how attached you have become. The queen isn't going to give you the Victoria Cross for reenacting Rorke's Drift with zombies as the Zulus, especially if you win but get bitten in the process. Consider it a zombie bug-out bag you can live in.

Location, Location, Location

You can have the nicest, safest zombie redoubt available, but if two graveyards and a coroner's office are only a few blocks away from it, you won't get to enjoy it for very long. Your zombie redoubt's location is an important factor to consider, and while you may have originally bought your home for the lovely view and proximity to mass transit, it may be entirely unsuitable for defense against teeming hordes of the walking dead. In most cases, what you

live in isn't as important as where it is located.

The most important rule when trying to survive the zombie apocalypse is that you stay away from large cities. The reasons for this are manifold:

- *High Population:* During the early stages of the zombie apocalypse, at the turning point where a zombie uprising becomes too large for the authorities to handle, large cities will still be very densely populated: skyscrapers full of apartments, condominiums atop condominiums, and businesses crowding every corner and street. Initially, this might seem like a scavenger's best opportunity for easy pickings, but the problem is that those individuals who did not immediately die of accident, attack, or thirst during the first few weeks of the zombie apocalypse were likely transformed into the undead. In other words, the more people living close together, the more zombies. You can't clear out Manhattan, Chicago, or Denver no matter how many guns you have, and it is foolish to try.

- *High Visibility:* The last minuscule remnants of a thinking mind that exist in a zombie's decaying brain typically keep it from engaging in suicidal activities like walking directly into a blazing inferno. But just as a zombie won't usually shamble toward an immediate and visible threat, it *will* go after something it sees as an opportunity for food. So even if South Boston started out fairly zombie free when the undead began to plague the living, it won't stay that way. The tall buildings and apparent evidence of living brains to consume will be beacons to hungry ghouls, and they will travel from all around to get there.

- *High Danger:* There will undoubtedly be survivors of the zombie apocalypse who are too stupid or bloody-minded to leave their homes in the big city. Most of them will not have read this book. Any of them who *have* survived even the first few weeks of the zombie apocalypse will, then, be very dangerous characters. By definition, they'll have to be: if privation and constant peril harden a person, then imagine what it must have been like to survive a month in zombie-infested Detroit. The suburbs and rural areas will have their own dangers that you will have

These are not good neighbors to have. (Illustration by Dierdra Olin.)

to deal with. Don't add to your risk factor by fighting for those last bottles of spring water with brutal, aggressive city dwellers.

- *Lack of Freedom:* Large cities will attract not only the undead, but also captains of industry, politicos, and other self-important types who will take advantage of any crisis to profit personally. As mentioned in Chapter 3, "Zombie Apocalypse Basics," these wannabe dictators will move immediately and aggressively to take control of any and all resources available. While living in a big city

under the rule of a "benevolent" dictator might be seen by some as a decent trade-off when compared to the danger of living outside with the zombies, in the long run it is a death sentence. Whatever personal freedoms you used to enjoy will be whittled away by the whim of a despot until you become just another bootlicker, jumping when he says frog and eating when he lets you. Your freedom was purchased with the blood of brave men who fought and died for your country. You owe it to them to not trade it for anything.

- *Lack of Armament:* Most large cities have entirely disarmed their inhabitants, first making them victims of violent criminals and then making them victims of hungry zombies. Unless you live in a cartridge manufacturing facility, your supply of ammunition will be finite. So to maintain an effective defense against the undead, you will have to rearm yourself with whatever weapons and ammunition you can find. In places where owning and shooting a firearm are illegal, the pickings will be very slim for this kind of scrounging. Just as you won't get rich by robbing poor people, you won't be able to arm yourself by searching Chicago for guns and ammo.

- *Lack of Nature:* Aside from public fountains (which have most likely been stumbled through by pathogen-bearing undead) and decorative ponds, the water supply of most large cities will be minimal to nonexistent once the electricity runs out. And, at least in the first few months of the zombie apocalypse, there will also be fewer fruit trees and edible animals to provide the traveler with ample sustenance. Bottled water and packaged food items will only last so long, and to get them you'll have to fight your way through hordes of zombies, groups of roving bandits, and the private armies of corporate honchos who have cordoned off a safe zone for themselves and their lackeys.

Less-populated rural and suburban areas are your best bets for long-term survival in the days of the zombie apocalypse. Remember that your first priority is to stay alive, and to do so you will have to deal with as few zombies as possible. Stay away from places where the undead congregate and maximize your food and water-gathering opportunities, and you can survive years, if not decades, in a zombie-infested world.

THE ZOMBIE SURVIVAL TEAM

Jean-Paul Sartre famously wrote, "Hell is other people." One of the largest and most ongoing survival choices you will make during the zombie apocalypse is whether to stay a lone wolf or become the leader or member of a team. A lone wolf only has himself to look after, himself to defend, and himself to feed: the day-to-day business of survival can be easier, so long as he doesn't run up against a horde of zombies too large to handle on his own. A team leader has more people to throw at a problem, whether it is a zombie attack or the acquisition of water, and his individual safety is at lesser risk: more people means more front-line soldiers. For most of us, the decision to go it alone or to gather allies is, in many respects, going to be a personal choice rather than a pragmatic one. It depends on your temperament, your connection to the community, and your attachment to the ties that bound you before the undead destroyed civilization. If you should decide to go it alone, I salute you and wish you the best of success. For the rest of us who plan to band together with our fellow survivors, there are some considerations to take into account. In the zombie apocalypse, the people you travel and live with make up your zombie survival team.

Team Size

You can't feed everybody, you can't protect everybody, and you can't save everybody. It doesn't mean, however, that you shouldn't help anybody. What you will have to do is work out an optimum size for your team, taking living arrangements and resources into account, and stick with it as long as the conditions allow. For instance, you may be fortunate enough to live in a relatively zombie-free area, full of game and potable water from springs. In that case, accepting new neighbors and members of your zombie survival team would probably be a good thing. On the other hand, you might find yourself barely eking out an existence in a harsh-weather environment, living on what few scraps you can scrounge from the nearby structures. The choice, then, whether or not to share your last can of Spam with a needy stranger is no choice at all.

Whatever you decide, make dead certain that you do not form a group large enough to attract mobs of wandering zombies, gangs of marauding bandits, or the hunting parties of local warlords. Zombies will congregate where the food is, and if they discover that food is where you are, you have become that most unwelcome of people: an undead magnet. Hide your numbers and never tell outsiders

As soon as possible, assemble a zombie survival team made up of people you trust. (Illustration by Rolf Harding.)

Choose your allies wisely. (Illustration by Dierdra Olin.)

how many of you there really are. Don't make your zombie survival team a target by seeming prosperous and numerous, and don't present an obvious threat. There will always be a bigger, tougher, or more desperate band of survivors than yours. Just as your zombie redoubt should be unobtrusive, your zombie survival team should blend right in.

The human factor is always the most difficult to predict, prepare for, and deal with, so go with your gut when deciding how many people you want in your team. We, as modern Americans, have socialized ourselves out of listening to our gut feelings, which is why so many of us make foolish mistakes and get ourselves into trouble. A good size for a zombie survival team is what you think it is. Follow your gut, temper it with your compassion, and you will be well prepared for whatever emergencies you and your new family may face.

Valuable Allies

The zombie apocalypse is, perhaps, the ultimate equalizer: race, creed, skin color, social class, religion, and political affiliation are utterly meaningless when faced with being eaten by zombies. We are all equally tasty in the eyes of the undead. When considering members for your zombie survival team, you should be pragmatic: every person you include must increase your survivability in one way or another. Everyone else is either a liability or a competitor for valuable resources. The end of the world is not a popularity contest.

Characteristics to look for when selecting members of your zombie survival team include:

- *Resourcefulness or Toughness:* This is arguably the most important trait there is. The most helpless and weak of us will have been taken out early by the violence, suffering, and danger of the first few weeks of the zombie apocalypse, so it's likely that the longer someone has survived these darkest of times, the more resourceful he is. Making do with very little is going to be a way of life for the foreseeable future, so it's a very good idea to surround yourself with people who are familiar with hardship and live by their wits.
- *Medical Skills:* Medical professionals, including dentists, are highly trained, usually highly moti-

vated individuals with skills that will die out, for the most part, when zombie attacks have closed down all the medical schools. These people are also less horrified by the sight of blood and other leaking bodily fluids than, for example, the average supermarket cashier or tax accountant. While many doctors can be quite arrogant and demanding, their skills and knowledge will be in high demand as long as there is one human left alive who needs treatment.

- *Weapon Skills:* Proficiency in zombie killing isn't something that just manifests itself magically. It takes practice, conditioning, and a small amount of talent. Members of the military, weekend warriors, martial artists, and firearms enthusiasts will have a much higher comfort level with weapons and their use than the average peace-loving person. When getting by might mean daily combat with brain-starved undead, shouldn't you ally yourself with a man who knows his way around a battle rifle?
- *Survival Skills:* Many of you reading this book will not know how to track a deer, make a woodland shelter, or pick a padlock. If you can't do these things, and won't take the time to learn how, then you should at least work with people who can. Survivalists and outdoorsmen may be few and far between in the twenty-first century, but their skills will be extremely valuable once the electricity and water stop flowing. Find a primitive-skills specialist and learn what he has to offer now, rather than trying to survive a long, zombie-infested winter through sheer luck and willpower.
- *Cleverness:* Some individuals might not have immediately valuable skills like gunsmithing or game hunting but are instead innately clever or talented in other, less-obvious fields of endeavor, such as engineering or mathematics. Your zombie survival team will benefit from an answer man: someone who has general knowledge, life experience, and problem-solving ability. Just make sure that your team isn't too top-heavy with useless academics, because many of them can't fight and won't try very hard to learn how. Nevertheless, don't refuse the services and loyalty of a highly intelligent person who has

simply had the misfortune of being born in the wrong century.

- *Hail-Fellow-Well-Met:* It is extremely valuable to have at least one member of your zombie survival team who is not only a good judge of character, but can also easily ingratiate himself into the good graces of other individuals. As long as you yourself are not taken in by a salesman-type of low morals and weak character, such people can be excellent navigators through the potentially dangerous waters of negotiation with other bands of survivors. Cash will become worthless during the zombie apocalypse, so barter and trade will be the new form of commerce. The value of a salesman, wheeler-dealer, or other like individual who can get a good deal on supplies, de-escalate a tense situation with hostile human beings, and serve as a messenger/go-between cannot be overstated. Note, however, that the walking dead cannot be persuaded out of anything by anyone, no matter how charming.
- *Character and Courage:* Not everyone you meet will be brave enough to charge right into the middle of a horde of slavering zombies, but it is still vital that you can trust the people you place in your team with your very life. Survival in the zombie apocalypse is difficult enough without having to watch your back because that new guy there seems a little squirrelly, the more you think about it. Every member of your zombie survival team must be courageous enough to defend himself and his fellows from danger, and trustworthy enough to stay on watch without sleeping or disburse food and water without stealing.

Of all these characteristics, resourcefulness, courage, and cleverness are the most important. You can get by without a doctor or primitive-skills expert, but your team won't go the distance if its members don't trust each other and won't back up each other in a fight.

Children, the Infirm, and Pets

Pragmatism must be your watchword, but don't let fidelity to it turn you into a monster. The survival mindset is uncompromising but not brutal or unfair. Let your conscience be your guide, so long as it doesn't turn into a suicide pact for your zombie survival team. Deep down, most of us know right from wrong. Balance that against your survival needs, and you can live a decent, moral life, even at the end of the world.

Any children unlucky enough to be born into and live during the world of the zombie apocalypse should be protected. There is no equivocation here. Despite their potential noise and difficulty, children are blameless victims, and your worth as a human being will be weighed against what you do or don't do for those young folk who cannot survive on their own. The elderly and infirm, however, are a much more complex issue. On top of the horrible dangers you must face on a daily basis, how much more risk are you willing to take on? Can you push a wheel-chair for miles down the road? What if zombies are chasing you? My only advice is that you do what you can without killing yourself in the process. Your zombie survival teammates are depending on you to not only keep them alive, but also do the right thing. Take each situation as it comes.

Most animals that aren't good for eating aren't good for anything else; so don't make yourself responsible for taking care of any dogs or cats. While a dog will usually try to warn you in some fashion if it smells danger in the form of approaching zombies, a cat won't. It'll just slink away and let you deal with it on your own. The advantage of having guard dogs around is far outweighed by the danger of them getting bitten and infected by zombies in a place you can't immediately see, and it's not as though you can just ask them if they're OK. The last thing you want is to have a contagious, proto-undead pet running around your living area, licking people and infecting them with zombie viruses left and right. Remember the end of *Old Yeller*.

People You Should Avoid

To reiterate, the end of the world is a great equalizer. All men and women are potential victims when the undead have risen from the grave. In these darkest of times, you may be hungry for human companionship and, in your loneliness, might be tempted to ally yourself with just about anyone under the mistaken impression that we are all brothers who have not been eaten by cannibalistic ghouls. Do not

The family pet may be cute, but she poses an unacceptable risk during the zombie apocalypse. (Illustration by Jennifer Larson.)

make this mistake, as it can very definitely be your last. Knowing whom *not* to befriend is at least as valuable as knowing who to trust in a world where the consequences of bad personal associations can be your life. Character types to avoid include:

- *Conspicuously Wealthy:* In your travels, you will no doubt encounter individuals who have gathered a great deal of material wealth around themselves, especially in objects that are no longer useful, such as cash or electrical appliances. They may have owned these things before the downfall of civilization or simply scavenged for them when local law enforcement was no longer able to hold back the looting. This kind of hoarding suggests a grave misplacement of priorities, and such people are unsuited for long-term survival in a world where wealth is measured in the value of your companions, the breadth of your survival skills, and the depth of your personal courage. Training a person out of this objects-first mindset is, 99 percent of the time, more trouble than it is worth.

- *Beautiful but Helpless:* Just as in the days before zombies destroyed the world, the terminally attractive will continue to trade on their looks and sex appeal to get by. Any of these types who have survived the initial zombie onslaught will probably have done so through the close association of a stronger, more resourceful partner who has taken care of her (or his: beautiful but helpless people come in both genders) many needs and whims. The weakness of character inherent in an individual who depends on beauty over brains makes her a bad choice for a team member *unless* she is also a people person.

- *Not All There:* The appalling stresses of living through the first few weeks of the zombie apocalypse may be too much for certain people, who will crack under the pressure. This mental instability may manifest itself in one or more of the following ways: compulsive lying, self-destructive behavior, catatonia, dissociation from reality, or constant terror and jumpiness. In an emergency situation, you won't have the time to properly counsel someone who has gone over the edge. Decide if this person's form of insanity is too dangerous to have around, and assemble your zombie survival team accordingly.

- *Excessively Violent:* The world of the zombie apocalypse will be characterized by horrible, frequent violence. You will have to defend yourself and your loved ones not only from the undead, but also any hostile human survivors. Some of your fellow survivors will become psychopaths, unable or unwilling to determine the difference between a shoot/no-shoot situation: they'll have permanently itchy trigger fingers. Violence-for-pleasure seekers and people with gigantic chips on their shoulders should be avoided at all costs. No matter how good at fighting they are, they will still put you at significant, unacceptable risk.

- *Hair of the Dog:* Freed from social constraints, many people will deal with the horror of the zombie apocalypse by drowning themselves in drugs and alcohol. A drink every once in a while isn't a bad thing, but anyone who uses booze as a crutch to get through the day possesses a fundamental weakness of character that can manifest itself at the worst possible time for you and your team. What if he can't find his tipple of choice? What if he risks himself and his gear trying to break into a zombie-infested drugstore for OxyContin? What if he's too high/hungover to fight? Too many what-ifs there. Don't risk it.

- *Other Zombie Survival Teams:* It's likely that you'll meet up with other bands of survivors during your travels. It can be very tempting to incorporate them into your team or allow your team to be incorporated into theirs. Though it is debatable, the rule of thumb is that you should never ally yourself with a team that you're not sure you couldn't defeat in an all-out battle. Every team will be different, with varying skills and personality types. The only zombie survival team you can trust with your life, however, is the team you're a part of. If you decide to let a smaller group into your team, remember that at least in the early stages, their first loyalty will be with their closest friends, not you. And if you merge with a larger group, the leader of that team may decide to put you and your allies on the front lines as much as possible to put his friends at less risk.

ZOMBIE GETAWAY VEHICLE

There will be times when just walking to a place, especially a distant one, is not the best option. Between Point A and Point B may be zombies, bad weather, rough terrain, or marauding bandits. You're better off in an automobile of some kind for the speed and protection it can provide. Even if you should decide to hunker down and live out the rest of your life in one location, you will still want to have some kind of vehicle for emergency purposes.

Choosing the Right Vehicle

It's possible that the car you now drive is perfectly fine for your current purposes. But the world of the zombie apocalypse presents unique difficulties that may be too much for your current automobile to deal with when push comes to shove. You can either trade up now, dealing with the expense until your creditors are all eaten by zombies, or wait to acquire something better once civilization collapses from the weight of the undead. Important vehicle considerations include:

- *Auto Body:* The larger and heavier the frame, the better. Don't drive a motorcycle during the zombie apocalypse: it's too easy to get pulled off by undead hands or significantly injure yourself in an accident. You want a vehicle with a heavy steel exterior, like a 1960s–1990s era Dodge pickup. Your automobile must be tough and powerful enough to withstand the impact of slamming into a fresh zombie. Smart Cars, MINI Coopers, and Volkswagen Bugs are entirely unsuitable, as are mopeds, Segways, and most sports cars.
- *The Glass:* Just as it's a good idea to reinforce the windows of your zombie redoubt, you should have your zombie getaway vehicle's windows laminated to withstand zombie fists and the small-arms fire of thieving bandits. Be aware that no amount of laminate will withstand rifle fire—rounds from a long gun will punch right through.
- *All-Undead Radials:* All-terrain and run-flat tires are excellent to have on your zombie getaway vehicle. The roads you will be driving on will be in serious disrepair after just a few weeks, and you need to be able to drive in all sorts of conditions without stopping to change a flat. You *do* know how to change a flat tire, don't you? AAA will be out of business once zombies have become the primary issue in daily life.
- *Gas Mileage:* Weigh your need to get a vehicle with a strong body against the availability of gasoline in the world of the zombie apocalypse. A heavy SUV can drive over lots of debris, but if you have to fill it up once a week, you may be setting yourself up for failure in the long run.

Driving in the Zombie Apocalypse

Even though the traffic lights will still be standing, the speed limit signs will still be legible, and the lines on the road will still be visible, traffic laws in the zombie apocalypse will no longer be relevant.

This will not make driving any easier, however, and there are certain difficulties specific to the world of the zombie apocalypse that you need to take into account before getting into your vehicle:

- *Collisions:* Your years of driving experience have taught you to do everything you can to avoid collisions, which is natural. You now must overcome the psychological block that keeps you from deliberately running into or over something with your car. While it can be very damaging to you and your vehicle to hit something larger than a hog, if the alternative is being trapped in a vehicle that won't give you many combat options, plow on through. Breaking this psychological barrier will require practice (not on live people) and visualization, but after the first time you've done it, it will get a lot easier.
- *Destinations:* The roads will be littered with abandoned vehicles, corpses, foreign objects, unidentifiable debris, and zombies, so be prepared to take an alternate route to your destination if the familiar way is blocked. What used to be a quick trip down the block to the local convenience store may have turned into a nightmarish obstacle course of shambling undead and broken cars. Don't take any route for granted: get street maps of where you are and where you're going, and notate them as necessary for future reference.
- *Velocity:* Because of the potential obstacles in the road, speed kills. The faster you drive, especially at night or in entirely unfamiliar locations, the more likely it is that you will run into a vehicle-disabling object like a fallen tree, demolished structure, or spike trap set by bandits. If you must use speed to escape from zombies, remember that the world's fastest living humans can only sprint about 25–30 miles per hour (mph). Zombies, even the running variety, are not natural sprinters, and their clumsiness will cause them to fall down several times if they are chasing you over a long enough distance. This means that you won't have to drive 90 mph to get away from even the fastest undead runners: an easy speed of 35 will get

you out of most zombie trouble while allowing you a reasonable amount of time to anticipate dangers in the road.

- *You Are the Target:* If a zombie sees a moving car, it will chase after it, not unlike a dog. Any sort of functioning automobile is an attractive target to the undead, and if you find yourself being chased even by very slowly shuffling zombies, put many miles between you and them before stopping. The sound of a ticking engine and the smell of burned gasoline are beacons to hungry ghouls.

- *Vehicle Damage:* If running into something the size of a hog or Great Dane can damage your vehicle, imagine what would happen to it if you slam into a person, even an undead one. So now, what if your path was blocked by a *group* of fresh zombies, all shambling toward you? You and your car won't get away from that impact scot-free. Even if you manage to plow through them, deal with the visibility-impairing airbag deployment, and find a clear pathway beyond, your zombie getaway vehicle may stop functioning due to damage to the undercarriage. The more things you hit, the more likely that you will disable your car.

- *No Dead Blood for Oil:* When the electricity goes out, the gas stations will likewise stop pumping petrol. Gasoline will then become a very highly sought-after commodity, even more than it is now, and once it's gone, you won't be able to replace it. Equip your zombie getaway vehicle with a hose suitable for siphoning gas, as well as a container you can use for fuel storage. Keep an eye on your fuel gauge, and don't run out of gas when zombies are right on your back bumper.

Alterations

You might decide that you want to alter your zombie getaway vehicle to make it more combat worthy by attaching bars to the windows, reinforcing the chassis, and cutting gaps in the body for murder-holes to shoot or stab through. Remember that each modification will change how your car handles and functions, and a change here may cause a handicap there. No matter how much armor you try to rivet to your SUV, you won't turn it into a tank. Focus on not putting yourself in situations where you're hopelessly surrounded by zombies, and you won't have to worry about plowing your way through them in a vehicle not suited to the task.

Other Dangers in the ZOMBIE Apocalypse

6

Zombies will not be the only things with which you will have to concern yourself during the zombie apocalypse, and, in many cases, they may not even be the most fearsome things you will encounter. It cannot be overemphasized that the world of the zombie apocalypse will be far more unsettling, dangerous, and baffling than you can currently imagine. Do not become so focused on shooting zombies and scrounging for bottled water in abandoned office parks that you find yourself unprepared for other problems that arise. While no book can account for every contingency, read the following pages and be flexible, ready, and vigilant. Your survival requires an at-all-costs mentality.

FORMER GOVERNMENT AGENCIES

Even though the U.S. Army will no longer be able to keep the public order when zombies have shredded the Constitution with their filthy, cracked fingernails, it doesn't mean that there won't be scattered groups of former military men, law enforcement professionals, and elected officials looking to regain authority under the guise of "rebuilding the country." They will be well armed, well trained, and merciless, led by the sorts of ideologues and power-hungry madmen who were

probably responsible for the zombie uprising in the first place. They will seize the more resource-rich and defensible parts of the country with superior firepower, and once they've set up a base of operations, will gain more and more territory through intimidation and force.

- *They Will Have Uniforms:* These uniforms will range from an individual patch on the shoulder to a complete outfit with emblems and badges. The unifying symbol will most likely be a flag of some kind that is slightly different from the country of origin. For example, instead of the U.S. flag of fifty stars and thirteen stripes, they may keep the red, white, and blue but change the fifty stars to one big star. Or they may have the stripes go vertically instead of horizontally.

- *By Their Names Shall You Know Them:* Most of the time, they will call themselves the *true* government, referring to all other attempts at rebuilding the country as illegitimate. As such, there may be many "United States of Americas" within North America. Most of them will make a pro forma attempt at maintaining the Constitution, but those that have entirely changed it to reflect a certain philosophical sensibility (like keeping people of a certain skin

Soon after the apocalypse begins, former military and police offers and government officials will begin offering their talents to "rebuild the country." Avoid them like the plague. (Illustration by Jennifer Larson.)

color out) will give themselves a new name: for example, the Federation of United States.

- *There Can Be Only One:* These fiefdoms will not be ruled by a senate, group of elders, or other governing body comprising a multitude of opinions. There will always be just one leader, whether he calls himself a president or general. He didn't get to be in that position by considering other people's feelings and concerns: he commands absolute loyalty and rules with an iron fist.
- *They Will Have Things You Don't:* In their locales, some of these "Little Americas" will have subjects with the skills and knowledge to turn the water and electricity back on. In other places, the power might never have gone out; mostly, these will be spots that get their electricity from hydroelectric dams or even nuclear plants. A brightly lit city in the darkness of a zombie-filled night can be a welcoming sight, but zombies will also be drawn to it like moths to a flame. In larger cities, they will also have creature comforts, such as food and, perhaps, some kind of Internet connection.

If you value your life, stay away from these fiefdoms. They are not much different from the government-run internment camps that may have arisen to keep the populace safe during the earliest days of the zombie apocalypse. Aggressive, hostile, and expansionist, their rulers will stop at nothing to get more power, and living under their rule will be a nightmare for anyone who values personal freedom. Anyone you see wearing a uniform bearing the insignia of one of these "Little Americas" is to be avoided. A bandit or gang can be run off, but a soldier who is part of a larger army represents a more persistent and significant danger. Don't trade or treat with them for any reason: just get far away as fast as you can.

BANDITS

Almost as dangerous as rogue former government agencies and their minions are bandits. Bandits are typically less well armed and not as organized, but they are more likely to rob, kill, and rape on whim. Their only credo is might makes right, and the only thing they respect is strength. Individually or in gangs, they represent the majority of the living humans you will encounter during the zombie apocalypse. Assume that everyone you meet is a bandit until proven otherwise. Simply put, a bandit is someone who survives these dark times at the expense of integrity and ethics. If getting by today means slitting your throat or stealing your last morsel of food, he'll do it. Types of bandits include:

- *The Silent Cutpurse:* You will never see this type of bandit unless he makes a mistake. Typically, these kinds of bandits prey on itinerant survivors, waiting for you to bed down before slitting your throat and taking your stuff. They're not interested in interacting with you; they'd rather not talk to you at all. You're just like a deer to them: you exist as a resource, nothing more. Most of the time, they live in hideouts near attractive locations, such as zombie-free suburban centers and game-rich rural areas. They'll know the ground better than you do and will use that knowledge to their advantage by setting traps for the unwary. If you live your life on the road, be extra-vigilant at all times and avoid any location that looks too good to be true.
- *The Backstabber:* A backstabber will meet you on the road or will knock on the door of your zombie redoubt, offering friendship or even supplies. He'll trade with you, commiserate, and might even fight a zombie or two alongside you. Once he's gained a modicum of trust, he'll strike. Usually, he'll just disable you to make robbing you easier, but occasionally he'll just kill you for the fun of it. In rare, disturbing cases, he'll knock you out so that he can entertain himself for a while by raping and torturing you and your family. Never turn your back on anyone who isn't suspicious of you and seems too trusting or smooth upon first meeting: he's obviously up to something. It takes a while to make a good friend or ally.
- *The Cannibal Family:* There will always be groups of people who, in times of famine, turn to cannibalism to survive. Cannibal groups

rarely last more than a year before illness or insanity ends their lives, but until then, they are very dangerous. Like silent cutpurses, they only look at you as prey, but in this case, they don't just want your stuff: they want your flesh. Much like the zombies they've begun to emulate, they cannot be pleaded with or reasoned out of what they want. Reflecting the sickness in their souls, most cannibals will be extremely unhealthy in appearance and hygiene. Cannibal families spring up during the early months of the zombie apocalypse, when all other available food has been plundered, and typically die out after the first or second year. Killing them is the only moral thing to do.

- *Gangs:* Presenting a great danger to all who try to live an ethical life in the zombie apocalypse, bandit gangs are itinerant groups of thieves and murderers who prey on anyone and everyone they can get the upper hand on. A gang can have as few as two members (one of which plays the helpless victim role while the other strikes) or as many as ten or fifteen, who execute ambush strategies against other travelers and homeowners alike. Think of them as zombie survival teams that have gone bad. They may have started out as gang members who fled the dangerous urban areas in the early stages of the zombie apocalypse, and simply continued a life of crime. Bandit gangs are very dangerous but can be run off by a strong show of force.
- *Scouts:* Many individual bandits you meet will be scouts for larger bandit groups, whether they are cannibal families or bandit gangs. They are motivated by fear and greed, so they can be scared away with intimidation and violence: you have to prove to them that attacking you will be more costly than waiting for the next victim to come down the road. What will kill a zombie will definitely end a bandit's miserable existence. If you prove to them that you will be just as vicious and merciless in defense of your person as they are in attack, then they will select someone else as a victim.
- *Trading Partners:* Bandits can be traded with, so don't immediately run and hide if you should see a single traveler or group on the road. If

you can observe without being observed, you already have the upper hand and can gather valuable intelligence with which to make a decision whether to meet with them. It might be that what initially seems like a bandit gang is actually a well-armed band of people like yourself: another zombie survival team trying to make its way through a dangerous and zombie-filled landscape.

VILLAGES

A village is a group of people who have planted stakes in a particular area and have decided to live there, come hell or high water. They are differentiated from government fiefs by philosophy and resources only. Most villages aren't interested in building a New America and probably don't have as many guns as former soldiers and law enforcement professionals. They can be just as acquisitive and dangerous, however, and live by a set of laws and customs that may be at odds with your own. There are several types of villages:

- *Oligarchies:* As mentioned in Chapter 3, some local community leaders may decide to become warlords and take over the cities in which they formerly held limited authority. They will be backed up by local law enforcement and even rogue members of the military who were initially assigned to the area to keep the peace. Most often they will be ruled by an individual boss, not unlike an organized crime godfather, but sometimes will be governed by a small council of like-minded former captains of industry. Oligarchies are always split up between the ruling body of haves and the working class of have-nots. Their borders will be patrolled and guarded by armed men, and they are rarely looking for new people to contribute to society. They *are* hungry for resources, however, and will occasionally send out raiding parties to prey on travelers and nearby unincorporated inhabitants. They can be traded with as long as you seem like a tough customer. View them as you would a Mafia family, with the same level of trust and suspicion.
- *Tribes:* Some bandit gangs put down roots, with

the leader of the group becoming a bandit king. They exist to rob and plunder; few of them are interested in farming and hunting game. They will be mostly primitive, focusing on what they can steal from others rather than developing a sustainable existence. They almost always live right outside large cities, making occasional forays into zombie-infested city centers to get supplies and resources. Given the opportunity, they will always try to stab you in the back. Raiding and thievery are their stock in trade, so avoid them when you can and kill them when they come after you. The toughest, meanest sociopath in the area—who doesn't so much govern as terrify the weak into doing his bidding—always leads them.

- *Religious Nuts:* Like-minded congregations will sometimes band together to live the way their faith demands. They can range from peace-loving Quakers to truly outré forms of Christianity. Some will send out "missionaries" who will kidnap other survivors to make them part of the church, while others will just live and let live, happy to be left alone. Religious nuts should be evaluated one group at a time: Mennonites and the like are excellent neighbors who will help defend the whole area from a zombie attack, while members of the New Church of the Truly Angry Jesus will go on raiding parties to find converts and plunder. Be careful, though: some tribes disguise themselves as peace-loving religious nuts to lull the unwary into letting their guard down. Reasonable suspicion will keep you safe, and it might turn out that those nice Mormon folks aren't so bad to live with after all.

- *Clans:* Some villages are made up of people who just want to live ethical lives at the end of the world and will band together for the sake of safety and shared resources. Some will be primitive, living off the land, and others will make their homes in abandoned towns, trying to rebuild a version of modern society. If your zombie survival team was to put down roots, it would become a clan. The vast majority of clans are welcoming once you get past the initial cau-

tion and suspicion, and will treat you fairly if you treat them with respect. Most clans will have an individual leader who is supported by a council of some sort, based on a form of pragmatic democracy.

LIONS AND TIGERS AND BEARS

There are well over a hundred zoos in the United States alone, and, once zombies have destroyed civilization, few humans will be left alive to take care of the animals within. Desperate for food and water, some of these caged beasts will escape into the outside world, while others will be bitten by the undead or eat the flesh of fallen zom-

An often unanticipated danger during a zombie apocalypse will be escaped animals from zoos and nature preserves. (Illustration by Martin Reimann.)

bies for sustenance and hence become zombies themselves. In nature preserves and national parks, the Parks and Wildlife Service employees will be too busy defending themselves from zombie attacks to contain the predators that live in the wild. Between stray dogs left abandoned by their dead owners, escaped zoo animals, and wandering local predators, the entire world will become a dangerous place for humanity.

The danger of a crazed zombie rottweiler or polar bear cannot be overstated. Undead or alive, a large dog or other wild animal will be the toughest adversary you can face. With more musculature around the neck and shoulders than the most experienced bodybuilder, a thick skull you won't be able to pierce except with extremely well-placed bullets, sharp teeth and strong jaws designed by Mother Nature for ripping and tearing flesh, and deep-seated combat instincts honed by starvation, do you really think you're going to stand tall and face a bear or escaped tiger alone? Such beasts are best dealt with using high-caliber weapons shot from very long distances. Consider also that most animals, even the undead variety, can run faster than you can, and if you climb a tree to escape, a zombie animal won't get tired of waiting for you.

When hunting for game, make sure that any creature you bring down does not have bite marks anywhere on its hide and never eat anything that isn't strictly herbivorous. That opossum or raccoon might look tasty cleaned and dressed, but if it's been scavenging in places zombies have been traveling through, it might be carrying a pathogen that no amount of cooking will kill. If your zombie redoubt is located in a rural area, be prepared to deal with zombie animals as well as undead former humans, and arm yourself appropriately.

THINGS THAT SHOULD NOT BE

Less likely but no less dangerous are other, more bizarre creatures you may encounter during the zombie apocalypse. Consider that the laws of physics, chemistry, and biology are more plastic than you previously thought, and what you once considered impossible might now be commonplace. The idea that the dead have risen from the grave to

eat the living used to be a fictional notion. What else might you be forced to deal with?

- *Mutant Zombies:* The pathogen nanite or chemical/biological process that turned humans into zombies might continue to mutate, creating more horrific monsters than existed before. The substance that caused the initial zombie outbreak is most likely an accidental side effect of an imperfectly performed scientific experiment. As such, there's no telling how virulent the pathogen can get. You may encounter freakishly deformed humanoid undead, insane with agony and hunger, or worse: mutated zombie animals grown fat and frisky on victim after victim.
- *Higher Undead:* If you find yourself in the midst of a supernatural zombie apocalypse, there is a strong likelihood that you will bump into higher forms of undead, such as vampires. What will kill a zombie will generally kill a vampire: catastrophic brain injury or decapitation. Other means of killing vampires include immolating them and driving a wooden stake through their hearts. Vampires are typically pale-skinned and stink of blood (blood is their very sustenance) but, unlike zombies, they are highly intelligent. Traditionally, vampires are said to be able to mentally dominate the weak-willed, transform into wolves or other animals, and perform amazing feats of strength. They may also have other powers that you will be unlucky enough to experience firsthand. Most vampires cannot abide silver, garlic, or Christian crosses, and burst into flame at the touch of sunlight.
- *The Unspeakable:* There may be creatures roaming the Earth that are so terrible to behold that you can go insane from the very sight of them. The worst danger of a supernatural or alien-caused zombie apocalypse isn't necessarily the damage the zombies themselves can inflict, but rather the end purpose the zombies represent: the utter destruction of humanity. Zombies are aimless aside from their desire for human brains, but, when directed by an outside force, they can become unstoppable. Unspeakable, unnameable entities behind the zombie apocalypse can include extraterrestrial monsters,

Much of what you have to deal with during a zombie apocalypse will be unspeakable. (Illustration by Carlos Machuca.)

demons spawned from the deepest pits of Hell, and extraplanar creatures of multidimensional provenance. Unless your preparations for the zombie apocalypse include counterspells, magickal charms, and high-level quantum calculations, encountering such beings may be the last thing you ever do.

When facing a creature, monster, or other entity you don't fully understand, run. Zombies, even as individual enemies, are difficult enough; a mutated, tentacled zombie mountain lion with eyes on stalks isn't going to laugh at you if you flee from it, and, even if it does, who cares? With limited resources and manpower, you are less likely to survive a violent encounter with a demon, alien, or undead grizzly bear than you are an entire horde of shuffling zombies, so don't try. Pick your battles with this in mind, and you will live a lot longer in the world of the zombie apocalypse.

Preparations for the ZOMBIE Apocalypse

7

The world of the zombie apocalypse is absolutely terrifying, but it does not necessarily spell instant doom for you and your family. Preparation, knowledge, and willpower are the keys to survival in any emergency situation, including one where cannibalistic undead walk the Earth. The material in this book is not intended for mere academic study: take this information, use it, and develop an exit strategy for when the end comes. The zombie apocalypse is not something that will just happen to other people. When it happens, it happens *everywhere*. Rich and poor, young and old, strong and weak—all of us will be affected. It is *your* responsibility to stand up for yourself and protect your family when the zombie apocalypse comes. No one else will do it for you. And it may be sooner than you think.

ZOMBIE BUG-OUT BAG

A bug-out bag is a kit of some kind, usually kept in the trunk of a car or under the stairs in the basement or in the hall closet, that contains items necessary for getting through the first few days of an emergency that forces you to leave home. Usually, a bug-out bag includes things such as cash, an extra cell phone charger, a GPS locator, and other useless bits of nonsense that will just weigh you down when the undead roam the streets. From having read this book, you will know that once zombies have taken over, money will become useless, telephones of all kinds will stop working, and eventually the satellites that broadcast GPS data will fall to the Earth and not be replaced. What you need, then, is a zombie bug-out bag, a kit specifically designed to get you through the critical early days of a zombie apocalypse.

Even if you have a well-supplied and perfectly located zombie redoubt, you should still put together a zombie bug-out bag. Zombies may overrun your redoubt before you can get there from work, for example, or the military may have turned your entire block into a smoking crater in their overzealous efforts to end the zombie threat. It's one of those things that you're far better off having than not, especially in quantity. Survival involves taking only those risks that are necessary. Don't fly without a safety net if you don't have to.

Contents of the Zombie Bug-Out Bag

When you read this list, you will probably be tempted to pick and choose which things you'll want to acquire and which you'll decide to go without. That is, of course, your choice, but consider that the relative inconvenience of being overprepared is

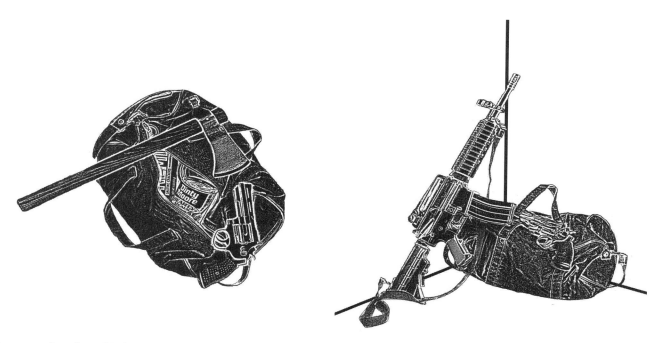

Two examples of zombie bug-out bags, one with a revolver and one with an assault rifle. (Illustrations by Matthew Doyle.)

much, much better than the dismay of wishing you had something you're missing. A properly stocked zombie bug-out bag will be expensive to obtain, but just like turning your home into a zombie redoubt, it will be worth it. You don't have to get all the items for it immediately: purchase what you can when you can, and eventually you'll find yourself excellently prepared for that awful moment when civilization has been destroyed by the undead. Items necessary for the zombie bug-out bag include:

- *Maps and Compass:* Get a map of not only your current home but the surrounding areas as well. You may have to travel for many miles to get away from the immediate threat. The best maps include topographic information so you'll know ahead of time if you have to do some climbing to get somewhere safe. Learn how to read a compass and plot distances and points on a map before necessity requires it of you. A supernatural zombie apocalypse might alter the laws of physics such that compasses no longer point to true north. In that case, depend on landmarks and the angle of the sun to point you in the right direction.

- *Guns, Guns, Guns:* Make certain that you have an extra firearm of the type you typically carry or practice with in your zombie bug-out bag. Also take along at least a hundred rounds of spare ammunition and, if applicable, several spare magazines. A cleaning kit wouldn't be a bad idea either but is not immediately vital.
- *Multi-tool:* Even a cheap multi-tool picked up from the display case near the cash register at your favorite builder's supply store is better than not having one at all. The better models include a utility knife and can opener. Failing that, at least get a Swiss Army knife.
- *Blade:* In addition to your utility knife, include a longer zombie-killing blade like a kukri or sheathed gladius. Don't worry about a sharpening kit now: you can always use rough stones on the road.
- *Flashlight:* This could be anything from a small, handheld LED pocket flashlight to a heavy Maglite suitable for cracking skulls. The caveat about using flashlights is that while zombies can't see in the dark much better than you can, they will investigate light sources they notice at night. Include extra batteries and bulbs.

Preparations for the ZOMBIE Apocalypse

- *Rations:* Take along at least four days' worth of food that does not need to be cooked to be edible. Make sure it's compact, like food bars or MREs. If you are at a point where you have to live out of your zombie bug-out bag, your situation is extremely dire as it is. Don't complicate things by putting a sack of rice in your bag that requires a good deal of water and fire to eat.
- *Water:* You may be tempted to bring along several bottles of water in case you find yourself in a place where such supplies are scarce, but don't do it. Water is very heavy. Only bring enough to get you through the first couple of days and include at least one self-filtering water bottle in your bag. Salt tablets and water purification tablets are also excellent things to have, as they don't take up much space for their value.
- *Fire:* Make sure you have waterproof matches, a lighter, and a flint and steel kit. While zombies will be attracted to the light of a campfire, if you freeze to death you'll be just as dead as if they'd eaten your brain.
- *First Aid Kit:* The risk of bacterial infection when living on the road is high, and you want to be able to bandage and treat injuries as they occur. Also keep extra supplies of any prescription medication you habitually take, as well as those antibiotics and other restricted medical products you may have been clever enough to acquire.
- *Warm Clothes:* Even if you live in a very temperate climate, take along a set of heavy clothes in case you find yourself outside at night without shelter. Warm clothes are definitely one of those things you'll wish you had if you forget it. Include extra socks and a hat of some kind.
- *Blankie:* A space blanket is a necessity. It can keep you warm on cold nights and can be used as a ground cover for wet surfaces.
- *Rope:* The uses of fifty feet of parachute cord or other such rope are almost endless, from building a shelter to creating a splint for broken bones to setting up a shotgun trap for blundering zombies.
- *Radio:* A crank- or solar-powered radio will provide you with a great deal of valuable information about the world around you, so long as

you use it properly. Don't believe what the government tells you, and, whatever you do, never go anywhere some disembodied voice on the radio tells you to.
- *Personal Hygiene Kit:* Baby wipes, deodorant, talcum powder, toothpaste, sunblock, toilet paper, a bar of soap, and a towel. 'Nuff said.
- *Shovel:* Also known as an entrenching tool or an E-tool, a shovel can be used as a weapon in a pinch, as well as a means of digging a quick foxhole in which to hide from zombies.
- *Armor:* Include a spare gorget and, if you have space, a pair of gauntlets at the very least.

There are undoubtedly items missing from this list that many survival-minded individuals would consider essential, such as a cookware kit, tent, and signal flare. During the zombie apocalypse, any structure not currently occupied by zombies could be used as a shelter, but the last thing you want to do is to signal someone and alert the undead to your position. Feel free to add to this list as your circumstances, skill set, and personal preferences dictate, but be aware that everything you bring adds weight. If you can pick a lock, add an extra set of lock picks. If you live in a cold climate, bring extra sets of warm clothes. Consider, however, that the worst thing would be for you to have to leave your zombie bug-out bag behind because it's too heavy to easily lug with you on the run.

The best place to store your zombie bug-out bag is away from prying eyes and curious fingers. If you are confident that you have a sturdy, secure zombie redoubt, then put the bag in a closet or cabinet in your zombie safe room. If for whatever reason you don't have such a place, then put the bag in your car somewhere under a blanket. Wherever you put it, it must be accessible, invisible, and complete.

After gathering the items for and storing your zombie bug-out bag, you may be tempted to sit back on your laurels and simply declare to yourself that you're ready: you're covered in a zombie emergency. This is one of the worst things you could do. Preparation isn't a goal—it's a way of life. At least once every two weeks, take a careful inventory of the contents of your bag, replace any perishable items with fresher ones and make sure that the electrical devices are still reliable. This exercise will help to keep you in the proper survival mindset.

ZOMBIE COMBAT DRILLS

Knowing *how* to fight is not the same as having the skills and attributes to defend yourself properly when zombies come pounding on the door. Knowledge without practice won't get you very far in an emergency survival situation, and if the first time you pick up a sword or a gun is when you're already surrounded by cannibalistic undead, you are probably going to die horribly.

Basic marksmanship and gunhandling skills are beyond the scope of this text to impart. It is incumbent upon you to learn how to manipulate and shoot firearms of various types, finding competent instructors to teach you. Embrace an exercise regimen that emphasizes endurance and the building of fast-twitch muscle fibers so that you won't get completely exhausted from a half-mile run away from hordes of shuffling undead. Just as the zombie bugout bag will help your material preparation, practice of combat techniques will hone your physical preparedness, making you a formidable foe to any zombie that crosses your path.

One way to build such combat attributes as speed, timing, and accuracy is to practice flow drills that burn battle-ready movements into your muscle memory. The more you practice them, the better you'll be. Don't get lost in the drills so that they become a kind of game: perform them with full intensity, visualizing striking down your undead enemy with each motion.

Blade Drills

Though the firearm is the preferred weapon for killing zombies, you may find yourself in a situation where you cannot shoot your enemy. Your gun may jam or run out of ammunition, or you might not even have one because of lack of preparedness or restrictive gun control laws. The drills listed here will require some athleticism and effort, but with repetition you will build functional muscle and combat endurance.

Never practice these drills in the air: always hit something solid, but not so solid that it won't give at least a little bit. Air performance increases the likelihood of your hyperextending your elbow and won't provide the tactile experience of hitting something good and hard. Striking something that won't give, such as a concrete wall or building, puts you at risk of injuring your wrist, elbow, and shoulder. A boxer's heavy bag, wooden post, purpose-designed human-like apparatus, or other such object is a worthy practice target. Put a mark on it with tape or ink at a spot that is approximately at head height so you'll be able to accurately pinpoint where you want to hit. Do not use live steel in practice: you can damage your blade, the target, or yourself with a bad hit. A dulled practice blade of good length and heft of the kind you plan to use in a real fight will serve you well in training.

Beheading Drill

One of the best ways to kill a zombie is to cut its head off.

- *Movement 1:* Perform a horizontal forehand strike, slicing through the target and rolling your wrist at the end so that the side of your wrist impacts the meaty part of your opposite shoulder.
- *Movement 2:* Perform a horizontal backhand strike, once again cutting through the target. Roll your wrist back when it feels natural to do so, and end up with your blade over your same-side shoulder, parallel to the ground. Use control: if you find yourself bouncing the weapon against your deltoid at the end, it means that you've just cut yourself.
- *Movement 3:* Pause and assess to see if you need to perform movements 1 and 2 again.

Cycling/Cutting Drill

A good, heavy blade can bisect a zombie's skull and cause a catastrophic brain injury, which should put its undead lights out for good. You will need a horizontal surface at head height to strike for this drill.

- *Movement 1:* Perform a vertical forehand strike, bringing your blade back at the end so that it is over your same-side shoulder, parallel to the ground. Imagine that your arm is pedaling a bicycle. Don't just use arm strength: drop your body weight as you cut through, and straighten back up at the end of the movement.

- *Movement 2:* Assess. Repeat movement 1 again and again as necessary. The faster and harder you train to do this, the more likely you are to kill a zombie with one strike.

Piercing Drill

If you jam the point of your blade directly into a zombie's eye socket with sufficient force, you can penetrate the thinner bones at the front of the skull and shear through its brain. Put a "T" on your target to show you where to hit at the eyes and nasal cavity.

- *Movement 1:* Start with your strong-side foot back and your blade held low at your hip, point angled slightly upward. Drive forward at the "T" with a forehand thrust, stepping *through* to create maximum force.
- *Movement 2:* Step back, keeping your opposite side foot planted forward while you bring your blade back to your hip.
- *Movement 3:* Drive forward again, this time stepping through with a backhand thrust. Try to get full extension of the shoulder and wrist.
- *Movement 4:* Step back once again, bringing your blade back to your hip. Only one foot moves through this entire drill: the strong-side foot. Assess and repeat as necessary.

Hack-and-Shank Drill

This drill combines cutting and thrusting to keep your undead opponents off balance. A good, hard hack into the neck may give your undead opponent a moment's pause (if you don't cut all the way through), which will lead into a thrust at its vulnerable eye socket.

- *Movement 1:* Start with your strong-side foot back and the weapon held over your shoulder, blade parallel to the ground. Step forward and perform a horizontal forehand strike, cutting through the target and rolling your wrist at the end so that the side of your wrist impacts the meaty part of your opposite shoulder.

- *Movement 2:* Roll your wrist so that your palm is up and your blade's point is facing forward. Step forward with your opposite-side foot while performing a backhand thrust. While you can generate a great deal of power by using your body weight to propel the thrust, consider that you have now brought yourself very close to your enemy. If the thrust only skidded off the top of its skull, you are definitely in range of its teeth.

Slice-and-Puncture Drill

If your vertical cut doesn't immediately finish the monster off, you can follow it up with a thrust to its eye or nasal cavity to pierce its decaying brain.

- *Movement 1:* Keeping the blade at your hip with your strong-side foot back, perform a vertical forehand strike, dropping your body weight to deliver maximum brain-bisecting force. Stay low at the end of the strike.
- *Movement 2:* Step forward with your strong-side foot, straighten up, and perform a straight-line thrust, using the full extension of your shoulder, arm, and wrist.
- *Movement 3:* Quickly pull back your arm so that the weapon is over your shoulder, blade parallel to the ground.

Zombie Handgun Drills

There doesn't need to be a whole lot more to shooting and killing zombies than centering your sights on the "T" of its eyes and nose and pulling the trigger. As stated earlier, you want to use the sights as much as possible, but that may not be feasible in extreme close-quarters situations. When selecting targets in a multiple undead situation, always shoot the closest zombie first and make sure it goes down before blowing away the next one. Focus on single, accurate shots rather than spraying and praying.

Failure to Deanimate Drill

Sometimes, one shot just won't do the trick.

- *Movement 1:* Aim for the center of the "T" and pull the trigger.

- *Movement 2:* Assess. If the zombie doesn't fall down like a puppet with its strings cut, aim and shoot again in the same spot. Your target is right between the eyes. As zombie movements tend to be slow, with their heads bobbing as they shuffle, you may want to err on the low end rather than shooting high. Don't waste bullets that just career off the top of its skull.

Undead Retention Shooting

When zombies are close enough to grab your barrel and bite the hand holding the gun, the last thing you should do is punch the weapon out at arm's length with both hands. This extreme close range is the only time you should ever point shoot.

- *Movement 1:* Rest the base of the magazine against your rib cage just under your pectoral muscle. This is the weapon-retention position. Cant the gun slightly upward and pull the trigger.
- *Movement 2:* Assess and shoot the same target if you have to.
- *Movement 3:* To shoot the next zombie, turn your upper body like the turret of a tank. This will take some time to master and get good headshots. Get a human-shaped target, place it at very close range, and after you shoot, determine where your shots are hitting. You may have to angle the gun a little lower or higher to get accurate shots. Practice hitting that perfect index point on your rib cage so that it becomes second nature. Don't look down at your gun when you fire; keep your eyes on the target.

High-Low-Medium Drill

Some zombies will be taller than other zombies, just like the people they once were. Don't practice to shoot only zombies that are six feet tall. Practice shooting zombies of all shapes and sizes, including ones that have had their legs so damaged that they can only get to you by crawling on their hands.

- *Movement 1:* Bring the gun to the weapon-retention position and shoot at a target that's directly in front of you at approximately six feet in height. Fire at least twice.
- *Movement 2:* Extend the gun out and shoot a target that's five feet away and three feet off the ground.
- *Movement 3:* Aim in and shoot at a target that's two yards away and five feet in height.

Combining Blade and Handgun

If you are adept at shooting with one hand, you can combine blade tactics with shooting to become a whirlwind of death to the undead. Practice these drills very slowly and dry-fire them many, many times before trying them out with live weapons. Each of these drills will have different movements, but all of them have the same two rules that must be followed.

> Rule #1: Do *not* shoot yourself.
> Rule #2: Do *not* cut yourself.

After practicing these drills for several weeks, if you still find yourself either muzzle-flashing your blade arm (pointing the gun so that your blade arm is in the path of the gun muzzle) or hitting your gun arm with the blade, you just might not have the hand-eye coordination necessary to perform these movements without causing yourself serious injury. Dying from a self-inflicted gunshot wound or contracting zombie pathogens from a self-inflicted gash from your own machete are extremely silly ways to go.

Always shoot with your secondary hand and wield the blade with your strong hand. There is great benefit to training to be ambidextrous in combat, but you must make sure your strikes have excellent power and accuracy behind them.

Shoot-and-Slice Drill

Intended for close-range zombie killing, the follow-up slice should finish it off if your first shot goes high.

- *Movement 1:* Bring your gun to weapon-retention position and shoot at the "T" of the zombie directly before you. In practice, imagine that the shot has gone high and merely cracked the top of the skull.
- *Movement 2:* Take your finger off the trigger.
- *Movement 3:* Perform a vertical forehand strike, using your full body weight to power the blow.

Your blade should bisect the weakened zombie head with little difficulty.

Hack-and-Shoot Drill

The blade opens the way, and the bullet closes the door.

- *Movement 1:* Perform a horizontal forehand strike. In practice, imagine that the blade has not completely sheared through the zombie's neck and beheaded it.
- *Movement 2:* As the side of your wrist impacts the meaty part of your opposite shoulder, step toward the side that you've just cut.
- *Movement 3:* Bring your gun up under your blade arm and shoot directly into the wound your blade has made. At this distance, it may be a point shot. For older, almost bloodless zombies, the vertebrae should be visible through the cut you just made.
- *Movement 4:* Assess to see if your bullet has effectively decapitated the zombie. If not, shoot into the temple to finish it off.

Shank-and-Shoot Drill

In case your thrust goes low and the blade gets caught, pull your undead assailant into the gun muzzle.

- *Movement 1:* Perform a straight-line thrust. Imagine in practice that your blade has gone low and under the chin or inside the mouth. It is now caught and stuck.
- *Movement 2:* Slowly pull your blade back, angling your weapon wrist upward to simulate dragging a reluctant zombie's head toward you.

- *Movement 3:* Bring your gun up to shoot through the zombie's eye at point-blank range. The overpressure from the gases leaving the gun muzzle may be momentarily disconcerting, as will the noise. Prepare yourself for that by practicing with a melon.

These drills won't always accurately represent the chaos and difficulty of a real fight against undead opponents. You might also want to practice hacking at zombie arms: to do so, have a partner extend a wooden staff at you from odd angles as you cut at it with a practice weapon. The more you practice cutting, shooting, and combinations, the better you will get at them.

Perform the drills under a number of conditions, including dim light, uneven terrain, and harsh weather. Most fights you'll be in won't take place at the gym or firing range. Train in the gear you are most likely to be wearing during the zombie apocalypse, including armor. You need to know how your body will move when it is encumbered by several pounds of protective steel or Kevlar. Doing the drills in a karate gi or in workout clothes will prepare you for combat only at the gym, not the street.

In practice, it won't take you long to realize that combat, even with firearms only, is an extremely tiring endeavor. Remember to never seek out fights you don't have to engage in: if you exhaust yourself too early, you might not have enough gas in the tank to get you through a zombie-infested night. Build endurance and strength, use proper tactics and equipment, and practice these and other zombie combat drills, and you will become a formidable foe of the undead.

Conclusion

The information presented in this book, all of it, will prove to be relevant to your daily life if you are lucky enough to survive the initial zombie uprising. From there, it will be up to you to survive the zombie apocalypse, when the undead have destroyed civilization.

No single text can adequately prepare you for all contingencies, especially events as catastrophic as the end of the world. Everyone's situation will be different, and everyone brings a certain set of strengths, weaknesses, skills, deficiencies, and prejudices to the table. Building your skill set to include combat-ready attributes, survival techniques, and bloody-minded willpower should be a constant way of life. As has been stated earlier, preparedness isn't a goal but rather a path. Your goal is to defend yourself and your family every single day and rebuild civilization so that those who come after you don't make the same mistakes their forebears made.

Like it or not, your survival *is all on you*. In these days of avoiding personal responsibility, frequent frivolous lawsuits, and increasing government interference in daily life, that is an extremely hard pill to swallow. We laugh at terms like rugged individualism, code of honor, and survivalism, considering them quaint and irrelevant. It's up to you to bring them back and install them into your very

character now, *today*, because when the world of instant electronic satisfaction, viral YouTube videos, hybrid cars, and 24-hour news cycles comes crashing down as a result of the mother of all "man-caused disasters," you will have nothing left but that.

Your greatest concern might be, "What if I go overboard? What if I change my life, prepare for the end like some kind of survival nut, and nothing ever happens?" Yes, appearance matters. And it can be very easy to overprepare and turn into a jumpy, paranoid psychopath. Survival preparedness doesn't have to be the only concern in your life. You have the right to be social, to get out and have a good time, and to have hobbies that don't involve shooting zombie targets and picking locks. But if you can find the time to watch television or go to the movies, you can also make time for your personal safety and ensuring the survival of your family. If you feel that you may be taking it too far, then you've probably taken it too far, and it's time to dial back a little. The only caveat is that your friends and associates, few of whom have seriously considered the issues you're making part of your daily life, may express concerns about your new habits. Don't let other people talk you out of being prepared for the end of the world.

Like it or not, responsibility for surviving the zombie apocalypse is all on you. (Illustration by Jennifer Larson.)

Grasshoppers always laugh at ants until winter.

I wish I could tell you that the zombie apocalypse might not happen, or probably won't happen in your lifetime. The timeliness of this text, however, cannot be overstated. Legal issues prevent me from revealing what I know about current and future undead-related events, but I can say that if you read this book, set it down, and figure that you'll make your preparations in a few months, you will probably be too late to save yourself when the time comes. Good luck.

F. Kim O'Neill can be contacted through his Facebook page: facebook.com/f.kimoneill.